Verena Lindenau-Stockfisch

Lean Management in Hospitals
Principles and Key Factors
for Successful Implementation

Diplomica® Verlag GmbH

Lindenau-Stockfisch, Verena: Lean Management in Hospitals: Principles and Key Factors for Successful Implementation, Hamburg, Diplomica Verlag GmbH 2011

ISBN: 978-3-86341-018-6
Druck Diplomica® Verlag GmbH, Hamburg, 2011
Zugl. Europäische Fachhochschule Rhein/Erft GmbH, Brühl, Deutschland,
Bachelorarbeit, 2009

Bibliografische Information der Deutschen Nationalbibliothek:
Die Deutsche Nationalbibliothek verzeichnet diese Publikation in der Deutschen
Nationalbibliografie;
detaillierte bibliografische Daten sind im Internet über http://dnb.d-nb.de abrufbar.

Die digitale Ausgabe (eBook-Ausgabe) dieses Titels trägt die ISBN 978-3-86341-518-1
und kann über den Handel oder den Verlag bezogen werden.

© Diplomica Verlag GmbH
http://www.diplom.de, Hamburg 2011
Printed in Germany

Table of Content

List of Abbreviations

DMAIC	Define – Measure – Analyse – Improve – Control
DMADV	Define – Measure – Analyse – Define – Verify
DOE	Design of Experiments
DPMO	Defects per Million Opportunities
DPU	Defects per Unit
ECG	Electrocardiogram
E-Health	Electronic Health
E-Kanban	Electronic Kanban
e. g.	for example
etc.	et cetera
ETC	Market Research Firm in Olathe, Kansas, USA (Elaine, Tathame, Chris)
EU	European Union
FMEA	Failure Modes and Effect Analysis
GKV	Gesetzliche Krankenversicherung
HGW	Heilmittelwerbegesetz
HR	Human Resources
ICU	Intensive Care Unit
IT	Information Technology
JIT	Just-In-Time
JV	Joint Ventures
KSA	Kingdom of Saudi Arabia
MIS	Marketing Information System
NHS	National Health Service
OR	Operating Room
PDAC	Plan – Do – Act – Check
PR	Public Relations
SA	Strategic Alliances
SIPOC	Supplier – Input – Process – Output – Customer
SWOT	Strengths – Weaknesses – Opportunities – Threads
TPS	Toyota Production System
UK	United Kingdom
UWG	Gesetz gegen den unlauteren Wettbewerb

| VSM | Value Stream Mapping |
| WSG | Wettbewerbsstärkungsgesetz / Gesetz zur Stärkung des Wettbewerbs in der gesetzlichen Krankenversicherung |

1. Introduction

"…I will follow that system of regimen which, according to my ability and judgement, I consider for the benefit of my patients, and abstain from whatever is deleterious and mischievous…" [1]

Whether this oath is sworn by future physicians or considered a moral guideline by nurses and other hospital staff: it contains the message that medicine and medical ethics follow economical principles (Schönermark, 2007). At least, they should. Astonishingly, waste is a common phenomenon in hospitals. Furthermore, the European healthcare sector cannot be regarded a cost-plus business anymore since hospitals nowadays have to cope with cutbacks in capital spending, financial pressure and reduction of staff. By way of example, the German health insurance contribution rate for public insured persons increased up to 15.5 % in 2009, tantamount to the rise of healthcare costs by 10 billion euros (Laschet, 2008).

In contrast, hospital leaders surely wish to design and maintain an ethical and economically justifiable system that leads to a win-win-situation for both the institution and the end-user: the patient. Accordingly, a more sophisticated approach that helps hospitals to work efficiently and effectively is needed. Among quality management tools, Lean is one suitable methodology that can help hospitals out of the dilemma.

Originally, Lean is a management methodology that goes back to production processes with the main aim to increase output by reducing input. The lean philosophy has its origin in the Japanese manufacturing industry and is strongly bound to the Toyota Production System (TPS). Toyota introduced this system in the 1990s with the intention to become one of the largest car manufacturers. Toyota's success is self-explanatory.

The following book introduces main principles of Lean and deals with the questions: what are the principles and key factors for successful implementation of lean management in hospitals?

---

[1] Abstract from the Hippocratic Oath, traditionally taken by physicians upon graduation, pertaining to ethical practice of medicine (Edelstein, 1943).

How does the lean methodology apply to the German healthcare sector and what are the main aspects to be considered to make Lean work in hospitals?

However, this book will concentrate on fundamental principles of Lean whereas general analysis concepts will be mentioned roughly but not introduced in detail.

Ideally, Lean is based on three main pillars: process optimisation, patient-oriented management and engaging and leading employees. Thus, each of the tree aspects will be centred.

First, key principles and tools of Lean will be elaborated whereas the importance of defining waste and value will be pointed out. Furthermore, new terms and trends such as Lean Sigma and Telemedicine will be of interest to show necessity and additional surplus to traditional lean concepts.

The second chapter is addressed to patient orientation. Hence, patients as customers are defined with regard to loyalty, whilst satisfaction and improvement measurements thereof are introduced. In this context, strategic alliances and hospital marketing are focused to show advantageous aspects that contribute to the improvement process.

Following, the third chapter deals with personnel policy to show interconnection between employee satisfaction and the profitability of a hospital. Thus, tools and methods to analyse and improve the satisfaction and motivation rate, such as surveys and auditing, are introduced. Most importantly, the role of employees for successful implementation of Lean will be elaborated.

Concluding, main thoughts and findings will be summed up.

2. Process Optimisation – Principles & Tools

Process optimisation is the first central concept of lean management to be examined in this book. This chapter deals with the main principles and tools of Lean to give readers an overview about the basic ideas of this management philosophy. So, the understanding for waste and wasteful activities will be enhanced and tools such as Kanban, Kaizen and Value Stream Mapping, that are helpful for identification and elimination of waste, will be introduced. Since Lean is a continuous improvement process, it is only natural that new terms and concepts arise. One serious new methodology is Lean Sigma – the synthesis of the two concepts Lean and Six Sigma – because it complementarily supports Lean by concentrating on error proofing and elimination. Lastly, the reader's attention is directed to telemedicine and e-health as these terms increasingly gain importance for the up-to-datedness in the healthcare environment of the 21st century. Eventually, new technologies can be implemented supporting hospitals to further streamline activities and to reduce costs.

2.1 Lean Methodology

Above all, lean management concentrates on waste and value. Therefore, managers must primarily be able to identify and understand the different natures of waste that appear in hospitals. Only this proper knowledge provides the basis for successful implementation of lean tools. Actually, there are two main tools of managing waste: Kanban and Kaizen. Both concepts have their roots in the Japanese approach of continuous improvement. Though, Kanban is about managing objects and production units whereas Kaizen concentrates more on streamlining processes and business activities. Whilst Kanban and Kaizen merely concentrate on waste identification and improvement, Value Stream Mapping additionally focuses the value aspect and the quality of outputs.

2.1.1 Cycle Muda

Muda is the general Japanese term for waste. It describes any type of activity that is wasteful or unproductive. In Lean, one furthermore distinguishes pure waste from non-value adding activities. As one of the core principles in Lean management waste must be identified, analysed and consequently eliminated. But what does waste mean in the healthcare environment?

According to Graban (2008) the following types of waste can be found in hospitals:

- defects,
- overproduction,
- transportation,
- motion,
- waiting,
- inventory,
- overprocessing, and
- human potential.

In general, defects are errors, mistakes or time spent doing something incorrectly. In hospitals, errors and mistakes might be wrong medication, wrong use of technical equipment or even a sponge left in a patient's stomach after surgery.

Overproduction describes any activity or process that is carried out without actual need. This includes extra capacity, service or time. Unnecessary diagnostic procedures with patients such as double examinations are just one example for overproduction in the healthcare environment.

Waste in transportation refers both to products and patients. Each time a product is unnecessarily moved the risk of damage, loss or delay increases. With regard to patients, transportation means the time a patient needs to get from one place to another. Among other things, this includes long distances between departments or even the way from the parking area to the hospital facility.

In contrast to transport, waste of motion means unnecessary movement of employees. Oftentimes, physicians and nurses have to walk miles due to poor or unfavourable facility layout and structure.

One of the biggest cost drivers in hospitals is the waste connected with waiting. This includes patients waiting for examinations or treatments as well as employees waiting because of workflow is not streamlined (e. g. physicians waiting for lab results).

Of course, waste can also appear in inventory. Excess storage and supply increase costs for handling goods or goods might get useless because of the expiry date.

Overprocessing refers to any task or extra feature that is designed to add value to customers but is actually not aligned to customer needs. One example is scheduling too many tests that lead to unnecessary waiting time.

Last but not least, one must also consider waste of human potential. This includes mistakes such as the failure of leadership not enhancing employees' participation in the improvement process. Further mistakes might be: not listening to ideas, not engaging creativity and respect nor recognising individual talents of staff members.

No matter what type or combination of waste might occur, in any case waste destroys value because resources are not allocated adequately. Lean managers must be able to identify any kind of waste or non-value adding activity because eliminating waste leads to cost reduction, better service, improved quality and improved employee and patient satisfaction (Graban, 2008). Only that knowledge background prepares leaders to concentrate on lean tools, such as Kanban, Kaizen and Value Stream Mapping, which will be examined in the following.

2.1.2 Kanban

Kanban again is a Japanese term and means card or sign. The main purpose of Kanbans is to show which work has to be done at what time to ensure optimal flow. Due to their physical presence these signs are somewhat self-evident or self-explanatory and belong to the pull concept. Thus, they are strongly related to just-in-time production (JIT). In hospitals, Kanbans are mainly used for ideal managing of materials (supplies and inventory) to avoid stagnation in delivery or wasted store-room. Classical Kanban consists of three main concepts: visual management, 5S principle, and standardised work (Liker, 2003).

The goal of visual management is to sensitise employees and managers to identify waste, problems and abnormal conditions and to reduce information deficits. Especially in a hospital environment with cross-functional work teams the use of signal signs or cards is estimated an effective tool to create awareness and to prevent problems. In the 21st century, many Western European hospitals already use electronic Kanban systems (e-Kanban) to reduce problems such as lost cards or errors due to handwriting. E-Kanban systems can be integrated into the IT-system of a hospital and allow for real-time demand signalling across the supply chain. The importance of e-health for lean management in today's healthcare environment will be further examined in chapter 2.3 Telemedicine and E-Health.

The second concept of Kanban is the 5S-principle. The 5S's derive from the first letters of the Japanese terms: Seiri (to sort), Seiton (to store), Seisō (to shine), Seiketsu (to standardise) and Shitsuke (to sustain). First, unneeded items are sorted out and useful items are kept according to their frequency of use. Second, items are stored according to the same principle. Items that are used very frequently (hourly use) shall be stored at a higher storage proximity than items that are used less frequently (monthly use) (Graban, 2008). The third S *shine* refers to keeping the workplace clean once chaos is abandoned. An organised workplace is then the basis to start with standardising procedures and conditions. In Kanban, Seiketsu plays a special role because standardisation helps to reduce variation in the system and increases patient safety. Furthermore, total inventory costs are minimised since trade-offs between high availability of materials and increased stocking costs are reduced (Liker, 2003). On the one hand, high availability ensures patient care or even lifesaving. On the other hand, obsolete or expired material such as disposables or drugs is unacceptable in a hospital for the sake of the patients' safety. After successful completion of the first 4S's it is important to sustain the reached level by frequent control and further supervision of the new situation to avoid falling back to old pattern.

Actually, Kanban is a simple method to maintain desired inventory of supplies while consisting of a visual and physical inventory management (Trusko, Pexton, Harrington & Gupta, 2007). As a result, waste is eliminated and avoided, patient care is enhanced and employees are engaged to participate in the improvement process.

2.1.3 Kaizen

Kaizen describes the Japanese philosophy of continuous improvement. With Kaizen, all functions of a business are analysed and all participants involved in the business process are focused. Historically, the methodology goes back to the Toyota Production System (TPS) and was introduced by Toyota after World War II with the main aim to increase productivity in the US car market. With TPS, all activities of the production/ process flow are analysed to find abnormalities and to eliminate errors by standardisation. But Kaizen methods are not restricted to productivity because it involves all members participating at all business functions within that production line. Thus, the method is contrary to the thitherto known command-and-control management methodology. Kaizen is especially suitable in hospitals because with that tool cross-functional teams can be delegated by vertical and horizontal management. Nevertheless, it is advisable to start with Kaizen merely in one department due to control and measurement aspects. The typical Kaizen cycle consists of steps known as PDCA: plan, do, act, check (Trusko et al., 2007). First of all, the current situation is analysed and problems are defined. Second, the whole process is displayed to everyone engaged in the examined process. Third, acknowledgement about waste and inefficiency is followed by action of improvement. Last, experimented improvement steps are controlled and measured.

In general, there are three types of Kaizen (Graban, 2008):

- point Kaizen,
- Kaizen events, and
- system Kaizen.

The determination of the three types complies with the scope of problems. At first view, point Kaizen seems contradictory to its core principle because continuous improvement is associated with long-time periods aiming at long-lasting results. Thus, point Kaizen refers rather to inventory and administration work than to complex and long operation processes. Actually, it does not take longer than some hours or one day. In hospitals, point Kaizen is therefore suitable for standardisation of administration processes.

In comparison, Kaizen events are used with a medium scope of problems and take some days or one week and longer. In fact, Kaizen events equal to the Japanese word Kaikaku, which describes the radical change or redesign of complete production units, chains or systems (Liker, 2003). This type of Kaizen is implemented in improvement workshops or events where people come together for a restricted period of time to find medium-term strategies or solutions. One example for Kaizen events in a hospital environment is the team creation within a single department or shift. In the past, cases of medicide hit the headlines in Germany, such as at the Cardiology Department of the Charité Hospital in Berlin (Reimann, 2007). Beside the implementation of anonymous letterboxes, a Kaizen event possibly would have been helpful to clarify abnormal high mortality rates in certain intervals and especially at night. Consequently, a trustworthy environment would have prepared the basis for nurses or attendants to commit assumptions and apprehensions in a subsequent and intimate interview with the ward physician or nurse. Thus, a Kaizen event might have provided a solution statement for or even prevention of the high number of medicide cases.

Eventually, system Kaizen – that usually lasts various weeks or months – refers to more complex problem solving and describes the classical lean transformation process (Graban, 2008). Ideally, it is combined with Value Stream Mapping to compare current and future state processes which implicates the focus on sustained success and continuous improvement.

2.1.4 Value Stream Mapping

One excellent tool to identify and visualise waste and to subsequently streamline activities and operations is a method called Value Stream Mapping (VSM). Addition-ally, VSM is a technique to analyse and measure the flow of material and information and to value how much each activity or operation, that is part of the value stream, contributes to outcome and total quality. In hospitals, VSMs are used to identify how long each step in a process chain typically takes and, most importantly under lean consideration, it measures the waiting time between each process step in the chain (Graban, 2008).

The typical Value Stream Map consists of the following steps (Trusko et al., 2007: 378):
1. Map the current state.
2. Identify process waste.
3. Map future state.
3.1 Identify new requirements.
3.2 Remove process wasters.
4. Implement future state.
5. Validate improvements.

Let's assume a hospital is facing problems with patient flow in the haematology department. In the course of lean implementation, the hospital management decides to create a Value Stream Map with the main purpose to find out the reason for daily bottle-neck capacity problems. First of all, the patient journey is followed from the beginning to the end and a visual representation of physical and informational flow is drawn. The physical flow represents every step a patient takes and the informational flow shows if everybody in the chain knows what to do next. The second step is to identify the process waste, which in this case is time waste. It is very important that all members of the chain are involved in the examination process and contribute with their knowledge and information about their routine functions and procedures (Liker, 2003). For better visualisation please see appendix 1 (page 67), in which a possible patient flow in the haematology department is presented. Third, a future map is drawn stating now the ideal value stream. Mapping the future state involves the identification of new requirements and the need to remove process wasters. For that, icons can be used that visualise which process steps are valuable, not valuable but necessary and which processes are pure waste and ought to be eliminated. Thus, the main objective of the future map is to create value by minimising waste (Trusko et al., 2007). With regard to the patient flow example, this means that process improvements are identified that lead to shorter waiting times between the single process steps. Once these improvement steps have been identified they can be turned into action. But, "it is important to recognise that some value stream problems cannot be fixed in the short term, due to cost, timing, or technology constraints" (Graban, 2008: 60). Although, Value Stream Mapping is an excellent tool that leads to immediate results it should not be qualified merely a quick-fix solution technique. Instead, it is important to continuously validate the improvements and to check whether the upgraded value mapping will be successful in the long run.

Value Stream Mapping is a core principle of lean management because it differentiates value adding activities from non-value adding activities and waste. Furthermore, VSM provides excellent information for improvement opportunities in hospitals either for rapid solution fixing or complex long-term operations.

2.2 Lean Sigma

As we have seen, Lean is an improvement strategy that concentrates on waste-free production and process optimisation. However, certain problems may remain unresolved or difficult systems and structures are too complex to be streamlined with lean principles only. This is the moment, when Lean Sigma comes into play. The concept combines Lean and Six Sigma methodologies. While Lean typically concentrates on eliminating waste and non-value adding activities Six Sigma is used to reduce the error rate and process variability (Trusko et al., 2007). With the combination of the two concepts considerable synergy effects can be set free leading to greater improvement that would not have been reached by implementing each of the methodologies separately. Following, typical errors that occur in hospitals will be examined to show the necessity for error reduction. Furthermore, Six Sigma will be defined and one of its core implementation methods will be introduced. Last but not least, the chapter is concluded by analysing performance measurements that help to make Six Sigma work.

2.2.1 Poka Yoke – Error Proofing in Hospitals

In hospitals, errors can occur due to failure of people, method or material/equipment. Errors due to failure of people include mistakes made by hospital staff such as nurses and physicians (e. g. wrong diagnosis), by patients themselves (e. g. overdosing) or by employees of external organisations (e. g. inadequate advice by pharmacies or medical supply stores). Errors due to failure of method may appear due to silo mentality (e. g. shift changeovers), power struggles and competitiveness among hospital staff; especially among decision makers such as senior physicians (Trusko et al., 2007). Errors due to failure of material or equipment result from defective devices and materials (e. g. outdated technology or even unsterile disposables). These errors are interrelated and interactive. In any case, errors in hospitals are regarded especially fatal because they harm patients' safety or lives. According to Graban (2008), errors in hospitals do not occur because employees are unwilling or incapable. Instead, most errors result from the complexity of the hospital system itself. Thus, errors are not necessarily caused by bad judgement, malpractice or carelessness. Instead, there is a need to understand the error itself to solve and to avoid future problems. And this method is known as poka yoke – error proofing. Poka yoke goes beyond simple corrective actions or extra inspection (yet hardly possible due to time pressure in hospitals). So, error proofing is an approach to understand the source of the problem and is therefore related to the Six Sigma methodology.

2.2.2 Defining Six Sigma

Six Sigma is a management methodology or statistical improvement toolkit with the aim to identify and reduce process variation that leads to defects. Developed by Motorola in the 1980's, it nowadays enjoys widespread popularity in many business industries. Six Sigma belongs to quality management since its objective is to perform at an error rate not greater than 3.4 errors per million opportunities (Trusko et al., 2007). The following table visualises how the sigma levels are allocated to defects per million:

Table 1 – Sigma Quality Allocation

Quality Level	Defects per Million Opportunities	
	Short-term	1.5 sigma shift
1 sigma	690,000	317,310
2 sigma	308,000	45,500
3 sigma	66,800	2,700
4 sigma	6,210	63
5 sigma	230	0.57
6 sigma	3.4	0.002

Source: own, following isixsigma and Trusko et al., 2007

As we can see, there are two defect numbers related to the levels of sigma in table 1. The figures under short-term refer to the initial determination of Motorola when the 6-Sigma-Programme was primarily introduced. After years of experience and subsequent statistical data collection, it turned out that long-term processes vary over time and the number of defects is therefore different to that of short-term processes. According to statistical findings, the 6 sigma level therefore actually translates to 2 defects per billion opportunities which signifies a variation between 1.4 and 1.6 sigma (isixsigma, 2008). Since hospitals are typically organisations with complex structures and long-term processes, it is advisable to consider the average 1.5 sigma process shift in the calculation. Provided that Six Sigma is implemented correctly, this also means that hospitals have almost zero possibility to commit an error exactly because of that complexity (Trusko et al., 2007). There are two main ways to implement Six Sigma: DMAIC (Define, Measure, Analyse, Improve, Control) and DMADV (Define, Measure, Analyse, Define, Verify). Whereas the DMAIC method is used to improve existing business processes the DMADV method aims at new process design. In the following, the DMAIC method will be examined since this method is more relevant for problem shooting in running hospitals.

2.2.3 DMAIC Methodology

Classically, the basic method of Six Sigma is divided into five steps: Define, Measure, Analyse, Improve and Control. Each phase has its expected outcomes and objectives that can be reached by certain tools used in the respective phase. This paragraph gives an overview about characteristics and tools of the DMAIC method referring mainly to information given by Trusko (et al., 2007).

The Define Phase concentrates on the design of an objective that is concordant with customers' demands and the strategy of the organisation. In this phase, the scope, benefits, time schedule and value proposition are defined, customers' demands are determined and a common understanding among all participants for key elements of the process is created. After the creation of a corporate knowledge basis, the project team can agree on suitable tools to be used in the defining phase to identify customer demands, to gain process knowledge and to define the problem.

First of all, hospitals are designed to provide service to external clients, primarily patients but also accompanying people and institutions. Additionally, internal customers – the hospital staff – must be considered. Suitable tools to identify customer demands are methods such as the Kano Model, an Affinity Diagram or a Pareto Analysis. Second, the project team must gain knowledge about the process to work successfully on the project. Thus, team members must become acquainted with many aspects of the process such as the purpose, details and key performance elements. Moreover, team leaders must be able to think in statistical terms. Appropriate tools to gain process knowledge are Process Mapping and the SIPOC Analysis (Supplier, Input, Process, Output, and Customer). Third, the problem itself must be defined. Two adequate tools to get to the core of the matter are a Force Field Analysis or the development of a Project Charter. At the end of this phase, every project member should know about the problem, key process elements, the time schedule and the organisation of the project, goals and objectives and the plan how to reach the target.

The main purpose of the Measure Phase is to collect and measure relevant data about current processes, to establish a baseline and to eliminate variables that are counterproductive. In hospitals, variable data include patient waiting time, duration of treatments and procedures, length of hospital stay, discharge, bed turnover time, parameters that are critical to quality and even hospital mortality. To develop basic statistics, statistical software programmes can be used to plot information about tendencies, variation or inconsistencies and even defects and process errors. Adequate measurement tools are a Basic Statistical Analysis, Random Versus Assignable Variation, Cost of Quality, Measurement System Analysis and Process Performance Measures, last of which will be examined in detail in chapter 2.2.4 – Performance Measurements.

After data acquisition, information is analysed to verify cause-and-effect relationships. In this phase, team members concentrate on the root cause of a problem or a set of problems while focusing on key variables identified in the measurement phase. Among others, key tools of this phase are the Multi-vary Analysis, Cause-and-Effect Analysis (also Fishbone or Ishikawa Diagram) and Failure Modes and Effect Analysis (FMEA). Given the assumption that most problems emerge from variation, organisations can use a Multi-vary Analysis to reduce the scope of problems by concentrating on the variation rate of a process. Here, one distinguishes between positional, cyclical and temporal variation. Data of the three variation types are collected and the largest number of variation within each group is identified. One will then concentrate on the highest-in-number variation to consequently reduce it.

The Cause-and-Effect Analysis is used to identify the source of a problem by tracing an effect to its cause. The creation of a Fishbone Diagram is a fundamental principle of the Six Sigma methodology because it helps to identify all possible factors that contribute to process variation. To create a meaningful diagram that leads to cause-and-effect identification it is important that all members involved in the problem-solving process agree on the final problem statement and contribute with their ideas and opinions about causes that are then added to the tree. The diagram first of all helps to visualise possible causes of a problem or negative effects and it can also be used as a brainstorming tool. Figure 2.A shows an example of a cause-and-effect diagram for medication errors.

Figure 2.A Fishbone Diagram for Medication Errors

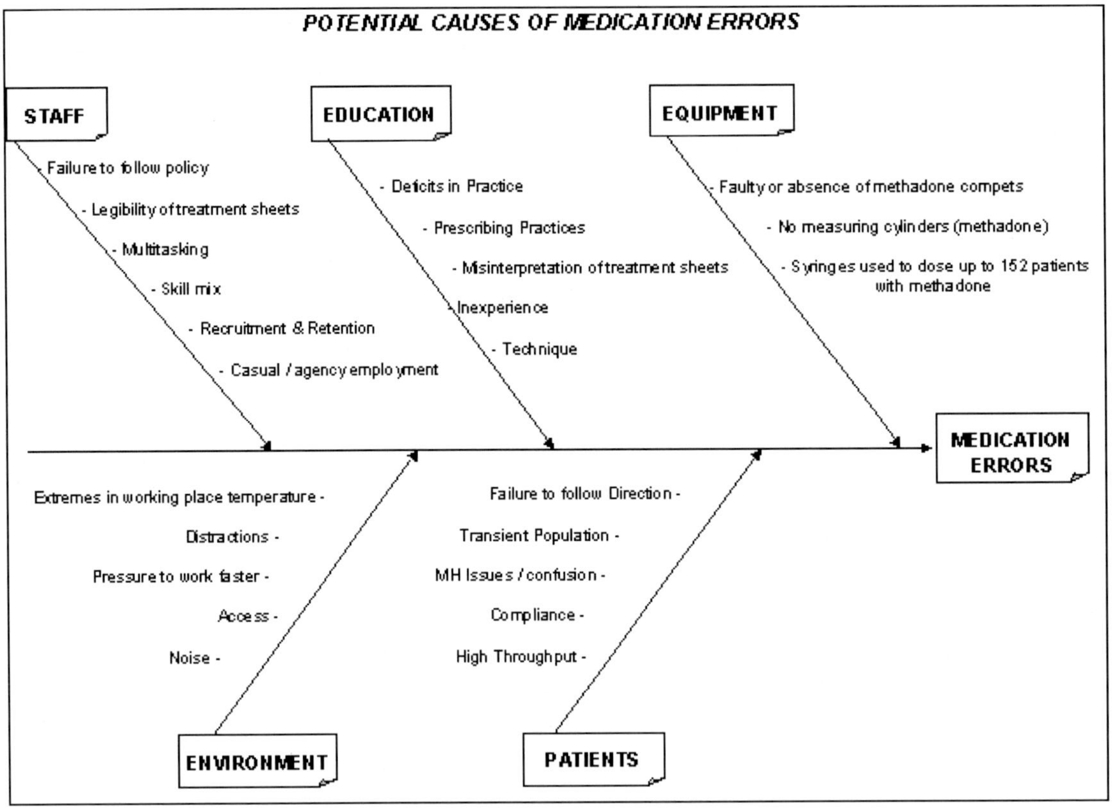

POTENTIAL CAUSES OF MEDICATION ERRORS

STAFF
- Failure to follow policy
- Legibility of treatment sheets
- Multitasking
- Skill mix
- Recruitment & Retention
- Casual / agency employment

EDUCATION
- Deficits in Practice
- Prescribing Practices
- Misinterpretation of treatment sheets
- Inexperience
- Technique

EQUIPMENT
- Faulty or absence of methadone compets
- No measuring cylinders (methadone)
- Syringes used to dose up to 152 patients with methadone

MEDICATION ERRORS

ENVIRONMENT
Extremes in working place temperature -
Distractions -
Pressure to work faster -
Access -
Noise -

PATIENTS
Failure to follow Direction -
Transient Population -
MH Issues / confusion -
Compliance -
High Throughput -

Source: Australian Resource Centre for Healthcare Innovations (ARCHI), 2008

The FMEA Analysis helps to identify potential failure modes and their frequency within a system, to evaluate their effects and to determine their impact on the quality output. With FMEA findings, hospital teams are enabled to estimate associated risks and their impact on patients' safety with the aim to reduce errors that lead to malpractice or death rates. The main objective of FMEAs is to eliminate the failure mode, to minimise the severity of the failure, to reduce the frequency or occurrence of the failure and to improve detection. Consequently, the use of FMEAs in hospitals leads to improved quality and patient safety, increased patient and employee satisfaction, reduced costs, wider knowledge of complex structures and processes, early elimination and risk reduction, and the creation of a positive working climate since team members are enhanced to participate in a creative idea process.

The purpose of the Improve Phase is to design alternative solutions targeting at further enhancement of the process improvement. Thus, new solutions are developed and compared whereas the best solution will be selected for optimisation of the process performance. To solve problems and to select the best solution certain improvement tools such as Statistical Hypothesis Testing, Comparative Experiments or Design of Experiments are used. The Statistical Hypothesis Testing is a method to validate a statement about a potential change. Thus, two hypotheses are set whereas one is about the expected change (alternate hypothesis) and the other one is about the remaining possibilities (null hypothesis). The alternate hypothesis can be accepted if statistical evidence proves that the null hypothesis is false. In hospitals, this method can be used, for example, to come to the decision whether to purchase state-of-the-art equipment or not. Whereas Statistical Hypothesis Testing is used to draw conclusions merely on statistical evidence, Comparative Experiments are used to evaluate real outcomes, usually with a two-sample experiment. In hospitals, this method can be used to measure the outcome of a clinical trial, testing new drugs or introducing a new treatment. The Design of Experiments (DOE) is a method that is based on experiments where input variables are changed whereas the impact of this change on the output is examined. Therefore, models with multiple variables can be designed to identify leverage effects for improvements and to determine disturbances. In hospitals, the DOE method can be used e. g. to examine the maximum capacity in an emergency room.

Finally, the Control Phase aims at maintaining reached process improvements and ensuring that any derivation from the ideal process flow is corrected before it leads to further defects and errors. With frequent control and observation, organisations have the opportunity to standardise new improvement processes. Besides statistical tools such as control charts, the Control Phase furthermore emphasises on continuous documentation, training programmes for employees, the creation of an open communicative atmosphere, business and management reviews, and the introduction of recognition and reward systems. These techniques and activities will help to sustain the improvement process, to challenge the status quo, to generate action and to drive further progress.

2.2.4 Performance Measurements

To make Six Sigma work there is a need for understanding the methodology's performance measurements. For organisations it is not enough to know about the concept. Additionally, leaders must understand the meaning of certain key perform-ance measurements such as DPU, DPMO and the sigma level. DPU stands for defects per unit and measures the performance of a product or service with respect to customer expectations (Trusko et al., 2007). In hospitals, a unit can be any activity such as patient registration, a treatment or surgery. DPU is the ratio of number of defects over the number of units tested. For example, if the registration time for 80 patients out of 100 is estimated too long then the DPU rate is unacceptable. But measuring the DPU rate is complex and tricky: only DPU levels of the same type can be compared. This means, you cannot compare the DPU ratio of a difficult 8-hour-heart-surgery with that of a simple hernia operation. Therefore, the DPMO (defects per million opportunities) has evolved. The measurement DPMO "is the average of number of defects per unit observed during an average production run divided by the number of opportunities to make a defect on the product under study during that run normalised to one million" (isixsigma, 2008). The formula is as follows:

DPMO = (DPU x 1,000,000) / Average number of opportunities in a unit

The DPMO is then translated to the sigma level already presented in table 1 – Sigma Quality Allocation. In hospitals, sigma levels can be used to compare performances of different shifts or departments considering all steps that take part in that perform-ance unit. If the error rate is different, analysing tools such as the Fishbone diagram can be used to understand the cause of the error.

For hospital leaders it is important to understand how to quantify performance (to think in units), to evaluate performance units (DPU), to determine improvement opportunities (DPMO) and to gain meaningful information that leads to six sigma level performance.

2.3 Telemedicine & E-Health

In the 21st century, it is impossible to imagine the healthcare industry without tele-medicine and e-health. But what stands behind these two terms? Due to rapid development of medical technology, there are many definitions for telemedicine and e-health (Norris, 2002); unfavourably and wrongly mixing up or equalising the two terms. Therefore, the first paragraph will give a clear definition of the two terms. Following, the various types of telemedicine will be examined to give the reader an overview about the scope of this medical field. Most importantly, it will be elaborated how lean hospitals can benefit from implementing telemedicine and e-health and which limitations still exist. Concluding, trends in the EU will be pointed out to show necessity and advantages for hospital leaders to get engaged with that field of medical application.

2.3.1 Defining Telemedicine & E-Health

It is hardly possible to find a single valid definition for the term telemedicine, mainly due to rapid development of technology in the fields of medicine and medical equip-ment. Literally, the term telemedicine consists of the Greek word *tele* meaning 'far' or 'at a distance' and the Latin word *mederi* meaning 'healing'. To complicate the matter, the term telehealth is used in an interchanging way assuming that telemedicine does not include aspects of education and services.

But the term telemedicine does not merely translate into 'medicine practised at a distance' because it would then neglect the mentioned progress of medical technol-ogy and information systems in the healthcare sector. Thus, it makes sense to further divide the term into the three concepts of telemedicine, telehealth and telecare which can be defined as follows (Norris, 2002: 17):

"Telemedicine is the use of information and communication technologies to transfer healthcare information for the delivery of clinical and educational services.

Telehealth is the use of information and communication technologies to transfer healthcare information for the delivery of clinical, administrative and educational services.

Telecare is the use of information and communication technologies to transfer medical information for the delivery of clinical services to patients in their place of domicile."

With those distinctive definitions the term telemedicine covers the three main aspects of education, service and care and further determines the roles modern telemedicine has to fulfil.

In contrast, the term e-health refers to healthcare informatics and medical electronic systems that enable easy and rapid administration and communication flow of patient data between healthcare providers. Thus, e-health merely deals with digital data storage and administration including IT solutions and Electronic Medical Records (e-cards) aiming at user-friendly and interoperable information systems. Telemedicine and e-health are two separate fields but they determine each other. For hospitals, telemedicine plays a more important role with regard to daily use of technology and medical devices. Therefore, the focus in this chapter lies on telemedicine as defined above.

2.3.2 Types of Telemedicine

As per definition under 2.3.1 Defining Telemedicine, telemedicine can be further categorised in four main types whereas information is transmitted as text and data, audio, single images and sequential images (video) within that categories (Norris, 2002):

- teleconsultation,
- tele-education,
- telemonitoring, and
- telesurgery.

Teleconsultation describes any medical consultation between two or more persons with the aim to overcome a spatial distance and to support clinical decision making (Norris, 2002). This type of consultation can take place between healthcare professionals only (e. g. cardiologists) or between medical professionals and non-medical people (e. g. physician and patient). Furthermore, one differentiates between real time and store-and-forward technology used in teleconsultation. A simple example for real-time teleconsultation between a healthcare professional and a non-medical person is an anamnesis carried out by telephone between an anaesthesiologist and an elderly patient resident in a rural area before ambulant surgery in a city orthopaedics clinic. In comparison, teleradiology provides an excellent example for store-and-forward technology. It is often used to transmit large X-ray files and to ensure information flow between medial staff and departments, such as the X-ray department and the OR.

Tele-education means distance learning using telemedical links to deliver educational material (Norris, 2002). Tele-education complies with the purpose of information transmission and the user group. Thus, distance learning can take place during teleconsultation, via the Internet or Intranet whereas users might be medical experts and healthcare professionals, students or private public people such as institutions and patients. One example for clinical education via Internet or Intranet is the digital library of hospitals or international interchanging education programmes among academic medical centres such as between the German University Tübingen and the Medical College in Jeddah, KSA (Becker, 2008). Information provided at websites of hospitals or health insurance companies, or forums about certain medical topics are only two examples of tele-education patients and other public persons have access to.

In comparison, telemonitoring is the use of telecommunication systems to gather routine or to repeat data about a patient's health condition (Norris, 2008). Thus, data between a patient at a distant location (such as at home or in an ambulance car) and the healthcare provider (such as a hospital) are transmitted through electronic information processing technologies. A simple example of telemonitoring is a blood pressure monitor or a portable ECG-recorder. The aim of such monitoring devices is to enable immediate decision making on a patient's treatment. Telemonitoring also includes data transmission of a surgery either in real time or recorded from the OR room to the doctor's office or to a lecture hall. Therefore, it provides new opportunities of tele-advise, tele-teaching and tele-learning. Common telemonitoring devices are diagnostic devices such as stethoscopes or vital signs monitors, imaging devices such as microscopes or ultrasounds and surgical devices such as endoscopes or laparoscopes.

Lastly, telesurgery or remote surgery refers to an operation executed by a combination of robotics and communication surgery. This way of operation is mainly used in microsurgery field such as prostate or inside vessel surgeries where manual human movements are too risky. The surgeon guides the surgical instruments via an interface at a comparatively short distance. Telesurgery is no more a medical dream of the future. Instead, this type of surgery gains acceptance among patients and is actually demanded according to Dr. Alexander Haese from the University Hospital Hamburg-Eppendorf in Germany (Ärzte Zeitung, 2008).

2.3.3 Benefits and Limitations of Telemedicine

After gaining knowledge about telemedicine and its meaning for hospitals it will be now of main interest how hospitals can benefit from implementing the technology and what are the advantages in a lean healthcare environment. According to Norris (2008: 30), "the principle benefits of telemedicine are better access to healthcare, access to better healthcare, improved communication between carers, easier and better continuing education, better access to information, better resource utilisation and reduced costs". First of all, telemedicine builds a bridge between healthcare providers and people who do not have easy access, such as residents in rural communities or elderly patients. Second, telemedicine delivers access to information physicians would not have been able to fall back on locally. Third, telemedicine improves communication between carers and delivers information that is more accurate, complete or timely. As an example, double examination and testing is avoided. Fourth, telemedicine covers educational aspects and provides an information pool necessary and advantageous for students, physicians and the general public. Last but not least, better resource utilisation and cost reduction are especially interesting in a lean context since waste can be eliminated and costs can be saved, e. g. demonstrated in digital teleradiology.

But telemedicine has certain limitations, such as "poor patient-carer relationship, poor relationships between healthcare professionals, impersonal technology, organisational disruption, additional training needs, difficult protocol development, uncertain quality of information and low rates of utilisation" (Norris, 2002: 32-33). Thus, hospital leaders must be aware that telemedicine can never be regarded a substitute but rather an additional feature that should be chosen and implemented deliberately. Further limitations are barriers of progress, which means users of the technology must resort to a common basis, such as infrastructure and standards, cost effectiveness, national policy and strategy, and ethical and legal aspects (Norris, 2002). In the course of creating a European Single Market, the EU has initiated the programme i2010 focusing e-health (euractiv, 2008). The aim of that programme is to enhance innovation, to create employment and to provide patients and healthcare professionals in all EU member states with user-friendly and interoperable information systems. This programme will surely help to align different infrastructures and standards and to harmonise national policies and strategies.

3. Patient-Oriented Management

One of the most important aspects in hospitals is the successful management of patients. This is true just because of one simple reason: without patients there is no need for hospitals. According to Daniel Jones and Alan Mitchell (2006: 16) from the Lean Enterprise Academy UK, "value under Lean is defined solely from the patients' perspective and everything that does not contribute to that value is waste and ought to be eliminated". The following chapter concentrates on factors that positively influence the bottom line in a hospital. Thus, patient satisfaction, strategic alliances in the healthcare environment and hospital marketing are of main focus since all these aspects are considered value-adding steps that help to increase service quality and to streamline processes in hospitals.

3.1 Patient Satisfaction & Loyalty

Patient satisfaction and loyalty have a considerable impact on bed occupancy rates which are actually the basis for a hospital's profitability. Consequently, it is this aspect of profitability which forces hospitals to increasingly direct their attention to patient satisfaction and loyalty. This chapter provides the basic understanding to classify the concepts of patient satisfaction and loyalty and how these concepts differ from those of common customers. For further illustration, the Shouldice Hernia Center in Ohio, Canada has been chosen to give an example of how patient-oriented management is put into effect. Finally, it will be elaborated how patient satisfaction can be determined by introducing the model of a satisfaction-importance-analysis as a suitable tool to gain information about the current satisfaction level among patients and resulting necessary improvement measures.

3.1.1 Patient Satisfaction – Distinctive Features and Drivers

To answer the question what determines patient satisfaction from general customer satisfaction there is first of all the need to define the patient as a customer. "A patient is a person receiving or registered to receive medical treatment". The word *patient* derives from the Latin expression *patiens entis,* pres. part. of *pati* 'suffer' (Oxford 1995: 1001). That is already what exactly distinguishes patients from common customers. Usually (except for plastic surgery), patients initially receive healthcare services involuntarily. Besides illness and pains they have to cope with strains such as with a limited private sphere, interruptions at any time of the day and night, long

waiting times, short-term rearrangements, limited influence on treatment and operation methods, stigmatisation, impersonal treatment and restricted maturity (Ziesche,
2008). Immediately, images of overcrowded hospitals appear, with patients waiting
for hours either before registration or even in their beds, sometimes half-naked on
the floors (Kusitzky & Schuster, 2008). Daily routines that help hospital processes to
run smoothly are perceived as impersonal behaviour of medical staff towards the
patient. Due to missing or unsatisfactory information about the clinical picture and
treatment methods, interruptions during anamnesis and examinations, patients are
left behind irritated, frustrated and afraid of their current situation. The feeling to be at
someone's mercy increases. All these factors contribute to limited consumer sover-
eignty. In contrast, the role of the patient has changed in recent years. Customers
today are strongly value-oriented. They buy results whereas the value of these
results varies regarding the type of service and the importance to the customer
(Heskett, Sasser & Schlesinger, 1997). In hospitals, the importance of the service is
clearly defined: patients expect highest quality of medical treatments and therapies,
and patient care is of existential meaning. Some of these factors (such as hygiene)
are regarded self-evident. Other service factors are estimated an additional surplus.
Therefore, today's hospitals are forced to develop successful strategies in which
patients are customers and healthcare organisations increasingly understand themselves as service providers. In the 21st century, patients have different expectations
of hospitals. They require higher involvement into medical decisions; there is an
increasing demand for understandable information and a strong desire for personal
rights' acceptance (Ziesche, 2008). Thus, it is indispensable, that patient-oriented
hospital leaders recognise the relation between patient expectation and patient
satisfaction. And this satisfaction turns into loyalty.

3.1.2 Patient Loyalty – How Patients Differ from Common Customers

Customer loyalty in the healthcare sector is different to customer loyalty in common
service industries. Patients generally do not re-buy this kind of service (except of
after treatment). And they do not wish to. Instead, they are happy to escape the
hospital environment. As a matter of fact, one cannot speak of customer loyalty in a
sense of maintaining customers or encouraging them to repeat their desire to buy.
More important are both positive and negative effects of word-of-mouth communication. This kind of communication is very credible because the patient speaks from

experience without any interest to repeat this experience. Furthermore, the leverage potential shall not be underestimated. Generally, satisfied people are likely to tell 5 to 10 other people, meanwhile dissatisfied people are likely to tell 10 to 16 other people (Ziesche, 2008). Thus, not only patients themselves have to be regarded potential communicators but also their family members, friends, other accompanying persons and visitors. An aggravating factor is that patient satisfaction is subjective. Hence, the evaluation of the medical supply and service is subjective too. All this leads to the necessity of carefully chosen patient satisfaction evaluation techniques. With a comprehensive and structured analysis, a hospital can determine its strengths and weaknesses, causes become transparent and corrective measurements can be set. Consequently, a hospital gains more latitude because management can react better and faster the more it knows about the patients, their expectations and the satisfaction level. For patients this means, above all, the improvement of the subjectively perceived service quality.

How can patient satisfaction be evaluated? Methods for patient satisfaction evaluation can roughly be divided into reporting and rating (Ziesche, 2008). For both methods it is important that the questions refer to all service dimensions in a hospital. These dimensions consider structural (framework), process (activities) and result (performing) quality of services in hospitals. Rating as well as reporting has certain advantages and disadvantages. Since rating enables patients to give differentiated answers using a predetermined measurement scale, answers are very detailed. In contrast, answers can be blurred by emotions and subjective sentiments. Reporting methods do not deliver such differentiated answers but the advantage of this method is that patients tell their experiences regardless of their expectations, personal relations or biases (Ziesche, 2008). The combination of the two evaluation methods provides a holistic approach for the measurement of patient satisfaction.

As in other service industries, the media of research are surveys, general and personal depth interviews, discussions and complaint management. Regarding complaint management, one must take into consideration that patients are not likely to put forward a negative opinion. Reasons for this phenomenon might be sympathy for oftentimes over-worked medical staff, fear or just displeasing feelings. On the other hand, especially complaints are real treasures for quality improvement. Therefore, an elaborated complaint management should be designed by the hospital management encouraging patients to contribute to quality improvement. Patients should be offered to participate either officially, giving them the feeling that their opinion is appreciated, or anonymously, installing complaint posts.

3.1.3 Shouldice Hospital – One Pioneer Example of Patient Orientation

One of the pioneers of patient-oriented management is the Shouldice Hernia Center in Ontario, Canada. The hospital management demands from its patients to learn about the hospital and its methods. As a consequence, patients are forced to deal with their disease from the very beginning. From the psychological view, the saluto-genic effects are of almost immeasurable value because involving patients into the healing process accelerates this very process. And this accelerated healing process positively influences the degree of a hospital's bed capacity. The model at Shouldice works as follows (Heskett, 2003): a questionnaire is sent to patient homes even before registration at the hospital. The rate of return is very high – 7 out of 8 ques-tionnaires are sent back to the hospital. The questionnaire then delivers important information to the surgeon who can now determine the whole operation procedure, which enables him to pre-estimate the length of the hospital stay and the after treatment. The surgeon puts all information into a database and sends a confirmation card to the patient who must return the card within three days; otherwise the patient will be contacted by phone. Only this procedure of 'pre-registration' and telediagnosis puts the hospital in a very favourable situation since bottle-neck capacities are avoided from the very beginning. Second, double-anamnesis and unnecessary waiting times are eliminated. When the patients arrive at the hospital, they have to wait approximately 20 minutes until a well-informed surgeon examines them person-ally to proof the already-registered information. Due to the information in the data-base this examination does not take longer than 20 minutes. Afterwards, patients are received by administrative staff who checks the health insurance coverage and who gives relevant details about the hospital routines. Following, patients are sent to the nurses department whereas they have to keep the luggage themselves. All patient rooms of the hospitals are semi-private, only containing two beds. Due to the ques-tionnaires, patients with similar jobs, backgrounds and interests are assigned to the same room. The admitting day ends with the dinner whilst nurses emphasise the importance of attendance because the dinner provides a great opportunity for all patients to talk to each other. From the very beginning of the hospital stay, patients are treated as customers. They have acceptable waiting times, find themselves welcome and respected as personalities and they are integrated in the healing progress. According to the operational theatre time schedule, patients are sent the next day to the pre-operation rooms where they receive the analgesic. Hernia operations can be executed with local anaesthesia. Hence, patients are offered the opportunity to follow their own operation and to participate via monitors. According to the Shouldice report, 99% of the patients accept this invitation. Again, the psychological effect is of immense value because this extraordinary information provides patients with security. Even one day after the operation patients are then encouraged by medical and administrative staff to exercise, to get more familiar with the facility and to take the opportunity to meet other patients. The programme at the Shouldice Hernia Center is an excellent example, how Lean actually is implemented, how it works and how hospitals can benefit from patient orientation. The whole registration and post-operation processes at Shouldice are streamlined; patients receive an extra-ordinary treatment considering involvement, information and respect of their personality. As a consequence, the hospital eliminates waste of time and patient satisfaction is very high.

3.1.4 Improvement of Patient Satisfaction

To improve patient satisfaction, data collection with the following final steps is necessary (Ziesche 2008: 104):

1. analysis and interpretation of information,
2. communication of the results, and
3. derivation of the findings and planning of corrective steps.

All data must be judged by its relevance, accuracy, currency and impartiality. The more precise data is evaluated the more detailed are the insights a hospital gains. Internally developed databases are real treasures and enable hospital staff to speed up processes without quality decline. Surveys deliver useful findings and the hospital learns a lot about its strengths and weaknesses. Consequently, corrective measures can be planned and processes can be streamlined.

One recommendable analysis method is the design of an importance-satisfaction-matrix. According to the evaluation data, two dimensions from the patients' view are relevant for creating the matrix: first, the importance of certain services and activities, and second the satisfaction level. Table 2 provides a simplified example of possible importance and satisfaction evaluation from the patients' view including structural, process and results quality dimensions.

Table 2 – Importance-Satisfaction-Allocation

		Importance	Satisfaction
Structural Quality			
1.	Accessibility	4	8
2.	Facilities	7	9
3.	Patient rooms	9	6
Process Quality			
4.	Doctor's consultation	10	7
5.	Attention of medical staff	9	7
6.	Waiting times	8	4
Results Quality			
7.	Healing process & results	10	6
8.	Aftercare treatment	7	4
9.	Administration	4	2

Source: own

The structural quality includes accessibility (degree of reachability, transport connection etc.), the hospital facilities (waiting rooms, cafeteria, toilets etc.) and patient rooms. Under process quality factors like the quality of the doctor's consultation, attention and friendliness of medical staff and waiting times are evaluated. Results quality includes healing process and treatment results, after-care treatment (family doctor, rehabilitation etc.) and administrative work (availability of documents for e. g. insurances). The data are then transferred to the following matrix.

Figure 3.A - Importance-Satisfaction-Matrix

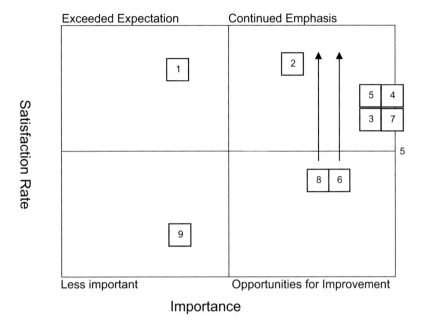

Source: own, following ETC Institute, 2008

The matrix visualises that from the patients' view, administrative work (9) is of lower importance in comparison to other factors regarding the results quality. Therefore, the hospital can save time and money by not investing in this part since patients do not consider this service a priority. The same is true for the accessibility (1) to the hospital, whose satisfaction rate exceeds patients' expectations. The hospital cannot do much about the location itself but it can be assumed that marketing activities work very well (please see also chapter 3.3 Hospital Marketing). Instead, further emphasis should be placed on patient rooms (3) (equipment and interconnection), as well as on the human resources component (4, 5) and healing processes and results (7). The data show that the hospital comprises a positive image of the medical staff and physicians. Previous investments in personnel policy fell on fertile ground and continuing emphasis will strengthen the hospital's profitability and competitiveness. More important for future improvement and corrective steps are the results of waiting times (6) and aftercare supply (8). Still, in these sectors there are opportunities for improvement. When targeting at improvement measurements, the hospital's re-sources and capabilities must be carefully evaluated. If those turn out to be insuffi-cient or unsatisfactory, hospital managers should think of alternative options such as the formation strategic alliances to eventually meet customer demands.

3.2 Strategic Alliances in the Healthcare Environment

A strategic alliance is a voluntary agreement between two or more independent organisations to cooperate in a specific business activity, so that each party benefits from the strengths of the other, and gains competitive advantage. Possible contract types of strategic alliances are mainly licensing, contracting and joint ventures (JV). In this paragraph, the following questions will be of main interest. Why is this form of cooperation interesting for hospitals? What are the main advantages, risks and challenges? What are the distinguishing features for a possible cooperation among hospitals and healthcare organisations? How do strategic alliances contribute to lean management?

3.2.1 Relevance of Strategic Alliances for Hospitals

To answer the first question, the German healthcare market will be analysed because it delivers important insights for the necessity to form strategic alliances. In recent years, general conditions for hospitals have changed due to pressure caused by regulations and reforms[2], demographic development, increasing financial pressure and the need for more transparency (Stanslowski, 2008). Especially with the introduction of lump compensations and further healthcare reforms boosted by the German government, efficiency and productivity have come to the fore and force hospitals to look for alternative structures and systems (Wende, 2008). Increasingly sophisticated demands and expectations of patients as well as higher mobility of the population in general require from a hospital to offer more specialised and diversified business activities to stand out from its competitors. A helpful tool to analyse the German healthcare market is the structural analysis of the industry according to Porter's Five Forces Framework. These five forces include the threat of new entrants (new hospitals, especially in the private sector), bargaining power of buyers (demands and mobility of patients), threat of substitutes (ambulant supply), bargaining power of suppliers (pharmaceutical, medical-technical suppliers) and the industry competition itself (rivalry among existing firms).

---

[2] See Orlowski, U., Wasem, J. (2007). *Gesundheitsreform 2007 (GKV-WSG): Änderungen und Auswirkungen auf einen Blick.* Heidelberg, Germany: Müller (C.F.Jur.).

These 5 forces result in a cutthroat competition within the healthcare industry and strategic alliances can help hospitals to cope with this highly competitive situation and to gain competitive advantages that would not have been possible without cooperation.

3.2.2 Advantages, Risks and Challenges

The general advantages of strategic alliances are share of investments, access to complementary resources, accelerated rate of return on investment, spread of risks and efficiencies through economies of scale, specialisation and rationalisation, and mutual decision making in the competitive environment (Albaum, Stranskov & Dürr, 2001). By forming an alliance hospitals can superiorly meet patient demands with regard to constantly improving treatment options and medical development (e. g. state-of-the art technology) and by aligning their service range to new trends and standards. Furthermore, the substitution risk especially from stationary to ambulant supply is limited and hospitals can react more flexible to changing environmental conditions (Wende, 2008). All these advantages lead to a better positioning of the hospital in the market and result in improved competitiveness. To find possible alliance partners, careful planning and a comprehensive analysis of internal and external conditions of the hospital is indispensable.

The first step should be the analysis of the hospital's resources and capabilities because they are the main sources of profitability. Resources are mainly divided into tangible, intangible and human resources. In a hospital, tangible resources are the financial backing and the physical (medical and non-medical) equipment. Intangible resources in hospitals contain technology in a sense of special treatments and the hospital image itself. Human resources refer to the employees, their qualifications, skills, commitment and loyalty towards the organisation. In addition, capabilities enable organisations to implement the resources. With the ideal combination of resources and capabilities a hospital can generate a long-lasting competitive advantage. Furthermore, a comprehensive analysis of resources and capabilities will deliver important insights to the hospital to identify core competencies. Weaknesses are even more important. The minute a hospital's resources and capabilities do not fit patient demands and expectations, but are necessary for the hospital to exist in the market, leadership must consider the option of any cooperation. Due to resources of partners core competencies can be created and competitiveness increases (Wende, 2008). But strategic alliances have certain requirements for success. So, key dimensions for development and investment into a partnership are goal compatibility, strategic advantage for all parties, trust and commitment, interdependence and cooperation, communication and conflict resolution, and planning and coordination of work.

3.2.3 Types of Strategic Alliances in the Healthcare Environment

As in other industries, the main suitable contract types of strategic alliances for hospitals are licensing, contracting and joint ventures (JV). In any case, choosing the suitable agreement type must be orientated towards the duration of the cooperation, relevant functions, operating distance and the number of parties involved (Wende, 2008). Hospitals have various options to form strategic alliances. The main types are regional, vertical, horizontal and diagonal alliances.

Regional alliances focus the necessity of a network that arises from political initiatives and practical constraints (Stanslowski, 2008). According to Geiger (2008: 34-35), "regionalism bears many advantages: cost reduction as well as concentration and flexible use of remaining budgets". Thus, contacts to expert groups are encouraged, regional opinion makers are more intensively bound, patients can be addressed directly and regional multiplier effects can be used. Possible partners can be found in the administration part (accountants), in medical and quality management (consultant companies), and in medical network (stationary and ambulant supply).

Vertical alliances can be found within the same business sector and refer to upstream and downstream value chains (Wende, 2008). This means networking of all partners before and after the actual hospital treatment, such as admitting physicians and rehabilitation. Further potential partners are social services, self-help groups, patient transport ambulances and emergency medical services, health insurance companies and therapists.

Horizontal alliances can also be found in the same business field but in comparison to vertical alliances they belong to the same value chain (Wende, 2008). Possible partners are hospital chains with one core centre or hospitals offering primary supply and further competence centres or specialist clinics. The main objective of horizontal alliances among hospitals and clinics are growth, maximised market power, increasing competitiveness and avoidance of waste, such as double performances (Wende,

2008). With horizontal alliances hospitals can meet the demand of patients by offering an improved service portfolio, such as special treatments and state-of-the-art technology. Furthermore, hospital alliances among hospitals are advantageous with regard to purchasing processes. Interconnected hospitals can built-up strategic purchasing which enables the whole hospital chain to reduce the bargaining power of suppliers (pharmaceuticals, medical equipment, disposables etc.).

Diagonal alliances can be formed between the hospital and companies from outside the industry (Wende, 2008). Potential partners are pharmacies, medical supply stores, laundries (in case the hospital does not have it in-house), environmental waste and recycling, housekeeping, educational organisations and consultants, mail and courier services, and even office supplies and vending services for e. g. cafeterias. Diagonal alliances will help the hospital to stand out from competitors by differentiation, which gains importance with regard to the upcoming wellness trend in the healthcare sector.

3.3 Hospital Marketing

Marketing has become a central issue for the existence of hospitals and healthcare organisations. In general, marketing includes all activities of distribution of a product or service. In a healthcare environment, marketing first of all means a philosophy or concept to focus the hospital's attention on its customers – mainly the patients – by using all resources, skills, products and thinking to understand and meet customer needs. With professional and correctly implemented marketing, interior and exterior hospital activities are streamlined and contribute to lean management. In fact, understanding the marketplace and designing a professional marketing plan will help to avoid inefficient and ineffective activities. Instead, valued resources (e. g. time, money) are identified and can be used in a more reasonable way.

3.3.1 The Market

The healthcare sector is subject to a variety of difficulties and restrictions and can therefore not be regarded a common service industry. This is true, just because of the following reasons: first of all, the healthcare market itself does not offer homogenous goods due to local, personal, temporal or objective preferences of the patients (Mayer, 2005). Second, "hospitals and health systems are affected by political upheaval; changes in government regulations; declines in reimbursement; the growth of alternative medicine; the rise of consumerism; an increase in competition from physician-owned specialty hospitals, retail clinics, and other business models; and a host of other complications" (Buckley, 2007: 6). In an international context, these factors must also be well-considered regarding socio-economic, cultural and legal conditions of the respective nation.

In the following, the framework of the Federal Republic of Germany will provide an example. In the 21st century, two trends can be seen in the German healthcare market. On the one hand, there is a fast-growing development of a private market for healthcare services. On the other hand, progressive liberalisation of the public healthcare sector can be noticed (Braun von Reinersdorff, 2007). Both sectors have to cope with difficult market conditions. In recent years, the German government has enacted various healthcare regulations and reforms with the main aim to increase transparency and to identify inefficient sectors (Busse & Riesberg, 2005). For hospitals, this results in important consequences regarding their market orientation. According to Mayer (2005), these consequences are mainly: cutbacks in public capital spending, decrease of overcapacities, deregulation of primary costs' coverage, intensive interconnection of ambulant and stationary treatment, enlarged reporting obligation and the introduction of a total quality system with publishing duties.

Furthermore, especially the public healthcare sector is restricted due to institutional interdependencies that originate from the German healthcare system itself. In general, patients are admitted to hospitals by physicians (either family doctor or specialist). The German association of health insurance companies controls and coordinates the compensation package and bills the provided performance to physicians, ambulant providers, clinics and hospitals (Mayer, 2005). These procedures result in two disadvantages: first of all, hospitals have to cope with inflexible billing procedures and, furthermore, patients lack transparency of the cost-performance ratio. The Euro Healthcare Index 2007, carried out by the Health Consumer Powerhouse, underlines that lack of transparency regarding patient rights and information (please see appendix 2). The index represents survey results from the patients' view carried out in several European countries. It consists of five sub-disciplines: patient rights and information, waiting times, outcomes, generosity of public healthcare systems and pharmaceuticals. According to the ranking, Germany has a clear need for improvement in the sub-discipline of patient rights and information because out of nine indicators 4 have been evaluated poor, 4 intermediary and only 1 good. For hospitals this means a real opportunity for quality improvement by adjusting their marketing activities to customer needs. When creating the marketing plan the above-mentioned circumstances have to be taken into consideration.

3.3.2 Marketing Plan

Marketing planning plays a key role in strategic planning and should not be neglected since it provides a guiding philosophy, gives inputs to the planners and designs strategies to reach objectives. As in other industries, a comprehensive marketing plan for hospitals should include corporate directions, a SWOT analysis, marketing objectives & strategies, a marketing mix and control & evaluation plans.

The purpose of a hospital and its *corporate directions* is clear and customers have distinct expectations and associations bound to healthcare products and services. Nevertheless, hospitals shall create a realistic, specific and motivating mission statement that fits into the environment and is based on distinctive competencies. Thus, the statement should not only be defined in terms of customer but also on employee needs. It is very important that employees at every hierarchy level understand the corporate identity of the organisation because this increases employee satisfaction and loyalty. Chapter 4 – Engaging & Leading Employees – will deal with that topic in detail.

To gain more information about their strengths, weaknesses, opportunities and threads, hospitals can use the classical approach of the *SWOT analysis*. Strengths and weaknesses refer to internal factors such as the mission & vision, financial resources, leadership, technology, staff expertise, quality commitment and the organisational structure. Opportunities and threads refer to external factors such as industry trends, competitive review and customer review. Optimally, weaknesses should help to concentrate on strengths, and threads should be seen as opportunities. Here, market research tools such as patient and employee surveys play an important role and will deliver insights that help the hospital management to undertake corrective action.

Marketing objectives are very important for the formulation of the marketing strategy. Companies must set definite objectives so the whole planning process can be designed. Hospitals deliver an unambiguous service to their clients and the main objective is clear. Common market segmentation can be neglected, or somehow appears at its own. Patients already form a distinct customer group with same needs, characteristics and behaviours. Such as in other industries, marketing strategies for hospitals include targeting, positioning and the market strategy. With regard to targeting tools, patients can be divided into groups with the most potential for the hospital. The clinical picture of the patient itself determines the need for the treatment, ergo the hospital. Hospitals should bear this in mind for their positioning strategy. One example would be a clinic specialised on orthopaedic operations and treatments. This hospital can differentiate its service while offering patients more value: expert physicians, specialised treatment, state-of-the-art technology, after-treatment such as physiotherapy & rheumatology, and even the location. So, the market strategy of hospitals is clearly differentiation – because with differentiation hospitals can offer patients extra value. This extra value must be communicated. A very helpful tool is the creation of a marketing mix.

3.3.3 Marketing Mix

In the healthcare environment, the classical marketing mix with its 5 P's (people, product, place, price and promotion) can also be applied. These 5 P's will be now examined in detail:

The first P refers to *people*. As already elaborated, it turns out that patients are primarily but by far not the only target group for external hospital marketing activities. Instead, accompanying people, admitting physicians, ambulant co-operation partners, health insurance companies, self-regulating communities, sub-suppliers, regional municipalities, potential donators and even medical journalists must be regarded potential customers for hospital services (Jahrbuch Healthcare Marketing, 2008). With regard to internal hospital marketing, the most important target group are employees because patient satisfaction is bound to employee satisfaction with reciprocal feedback effects.

The *product* in hospitals is a service that consists of core and additional medical and non-medical performances that must be adjusted to customer expectations and demands (Mayer, 2005). Thus, a comprehensive marketing information system (MIS) that delivers needed, timely and accurate information about all members of the target group will help marketing decision makers. The main functions of such a MIS are to assess marketing information needs, to develop and help analysing needed information and to distribute and use information. From this information-based point of view, hospitals can decide about possible activity areas. According to Mayer (2005), these activity areas include measurements regarding performance innovation, variation, elimination and differentiation. Hospitals can improve their image and gain competitive advantage by purchasing state-of-the art technology, offering alternative treatment options, reducing waiting times and diversifying their service portfolio offering patients value-adding performances such as wellness activities that accelerate the healing process. Additionally, key healthcare trends such as technology, lifestyle, prevention and communication should find consideration in the non-medical activity areas of the hospital (Müller, Kossack & Gröfke, 2008). One example might be precautionary fitness activities for patients and accompanying persons in an in-house gym in co-operation with and backed-up by financial support programmes of health insurance companies.

Place in hospital services means physical, temporal, informational, acquisitive and psychological accessibility (Mayer, 2005). The physical dimension refers to the infrastructure of a hospital. Especially in rural areas, transport connections are limited and hospitals might think about possible remedy such as shuttle services. This situation provides a good example how strategic alliances might come into play. The temporal dimension includes aspects like closeness to the facility and surgery hours. Particularly, specialist clinics should think about extended opening hours. As an example, the possibility of a Friday afternoon or Saturday morning consultation at an in-house gynaecologist will surely be appreciated by working women. The informational accessibility is bound to public relations of the hospital. Since professional PR is as complex as important It wlll be worked out more detailcd in the paragraph *Promotion*. The acquisitive dimension refers to the distributing channels. Supply channels in hospitals are downstream, with marketing channel partners such as admitting physicians who link the hospital with its patients. According to the already described structure of the German healthcare system hospitals do not have alternatives to avoid admitting channel members and should therefore especially concentrate on those regarding the PR work. Therefore, a vertical marketing system must be aimed at with all channel members acting in a unified system. The psychological dimension applies to the creation of a mental and emotional accessibility for patients. Here, the interior design of the hospital and soft skills of the medical staff will help increasing consumer satisfaction and loyalty.

The next P to be considered is the *price*. For many years, the German healthcare sector has been solely a cost-plus pricing sector. Hospitals had two formal objectives: maintenance of assets value and liquidity (Mayer, 2005). In the course of liberalisation of the healthcare market, competitiveness, as a third objective, gains more and more importance. In Germany, remuneration of healthcare performances is generally controlled and coordinated by the German legal association of health insurance companies (GKV). Hospitals can make a virtue out of necessity by publishing quality data (for example in the Internet) to increase quality transparency demanded from the governmental side. This improvement of quality transparency will also give patients the desired information about the cost-performance ratio. In contrast to patients with public healthcare insurance, this might result in a competitive advantage for private patients because this customer group will focus more on the cost-performance ratio of the primary healthcare, whereas public patients regard this self-evident. Beside these *hidden* prices (since coordinated by the GKV) there are also real prices and additional conditions (Mayer, 2005). Real costs mainly include additional payment (such as for medication), transport costs, payment for parking areas but also opportunity costs like inactive periods due to sick leave especially freelancers or salaried employees are constrained with after a certain time. Additional conditions refer to the expenditure of time, diagnosis and therapy and even the walking time from the parking area to the hospital facility (which is especially important for elderly or disabled people). Therefore, only psychological or promotional pricing are applicable price-adjustment strategies for hospitals.

The last P refers to *promotion*. The main aim of service marketing in hospitals is to visualise immaterial services to increase positive quality associations and creditability among the target group (Jahrbuch Healthcare Marketing, 2008). But promotional activities at hospitals are restricted by German laws on advertising in the healthcare sector. Among other things, the German Act on Drugs and Healthcare Advertising (Heilmittelwerbegesetz, HWG) has the aim to protect non-experts from irrelevant, misleading, manipulative advertising messages and from stimulation of improper self-healing attempts. The German Act against Unfair Practices (Gesetz gegen den unlauteren Wettbewerb, UWG) prohibits certain trade activities that lead to unfair competition and that violate morality. Furthermore, physicians are bound to professional regulations and ethics that prohibit especially promoting, misleading and comparative advertising activities according to § 27 of the Medical Association's professional code of conduct (Bundesärztekammer, 2008). This code of conduct disables physicians to use advertising for personal economical benefits. Though, in the course of creating a European Single Market it should be checked if and how these regulations can be conciliated with the European Law since there might be legal possibilities for hospitals to overcome some restrictions. However, the professional and healthy relationship with journalists is interesting because expert literature and regional media are of special importance to overcome advertising restrictions. Although the promotion mix in the healthcare sector is limited by the above-mentioned laws, hospitals cannot afford to abstain from marketing communication elements (advertising, sales promotion, public relations, direct mailing and personal selling) that are important for the competitiveness of the hospital.

3.3.4 Control & Evaluation Plans

Marketing is a dynamic process that needs continuous control and evaluation. Hospitals ask for a simultaneous implementation of horizontal and vertical marketing activities. Horizontal implementation refers to internal and external dimensions as well as to inside and outside dimensions (Mayer, 2005). This means that hospital managers must know about the necessity to concentrate on both internal and external marketing activities because they are mutually dependant and bear synergy effects. Inside-outside dimensions, and vice versa, mean that these internal and external factors influence each other and must be observed and evaluated simultaneously. Vertical implementation refers to all hierarchy levels of the hospital. It is very important that every member of the hospital staff at every level is involved in the improvement process. No one else but front-line employees, such as nurses, know best about all strong and weak points of work processes at the department. On the other hand, control and corrective measures must always be initiated from the management. Thus, top-down implementation and vice versa shall be considered at the same time. Hospital managers must include these interactions in their marketing considerations to ensure a professional and holistic approach towards their marketing activities.

4. Engaging & Leading Employees

Lean is not only about process optimisation and patient-oriented management. "Yet, for Lean to work, it needs the active, enthusiastic cooperation of staff" (Jones & Mitchell, 2006: 21). The lean concept, whose core statement is actually to achieve higher outputs while streamlining inputs, inadvertently provokes the assumption of a negative personnel policy that is determined by increased workload or even redundancies. This is not precisely how Lean works. Instead, lean management calls for a reflected interaction with employees. Following, it will be elaborated why and how employee satisfaction and motivation contribute to a sound and proper basis for smooth implementation of lean processes. Furthermore, employee attitude surveys will be of interest to show hospital managers a suitable way for a situational analysis and problem identification. But knowing about a company's strengths and weaknesses with first-hand information from employees is just one side of the coin. The other side is how to use the survey findings and effectively exploit them for corrective measures and further steps towards a lean hospital. Hence, the last chapter of this paragraph deals with auditing which is one tool for successful realisation of process optimisation while concentrating on the human aspect likewise.

4.1 Employee Satisfaction & Motivation

The level of employee satisfaction and motivation considerably influences the profitability of a company. This is especially true for variable costs, such as labour costs. According to Lewis, (2001: 14-15) "these variable costs include high supervisor-to-worker-ratios, training time, on-the-job injuries, sick days, absenteeism, employee turnover, daily productivity standards, percentage of work, low-quality output or substandard work and countless other issues that have an impact on the costs of doing business." This paragraph deals with the importance of employee satisfaction and motivation and its impact on the work performance. Furthermore, skills and abilities will be examined that generally support managers in their executive functions and specifically contribute to successful employee motivation. Most importantly, it will be elaborated what determines the motivational level of staff and how managers can increase it. Lastly, conflict resolution as one managerial tool will be elaborated because conflicts bear high risks to poison the working climate and therefore destroy satisfaction and motivation among staff.

4.1.1 Role of Employee Satisfaction & Motivation

In many companies, especially service providers, employees are the backbone for successful operation. Without motivated employees even most sophisticated processes and techniques will not tap their full potential. In the past, medical engineering has been overemphasised in hospitals while the focus on human capital has been neglected (Braun von Reinersdorff, 2007). This is surprising since the healthcare sector is one of the industries with the highest personnel intensity. Actually, the human resources (HR) management should have been centred automatically just because of two simple reasons: first, the human factor is the biggest cost factor in hospitals.

In general, labour costs come up to 60 to 70 % of the overall costs (Braun von Reinersdorff, 2007). Therefore, personnel management should be of prior interest since motivated and satisfied employees contribute significantly to a company's success and profitability. Furthermore, an ideal human resources management limits high turnover rates that cost companies a fortune. Second, high personnel intensity implicates a high leverage effect on performances. In lean hospitals this is especially true with regard to optimisation and interaction potentials. Hospitals with unmotivated, frustrated employees whose needs and demands have been ignored in the long run can easily face problems with sabotage such as retard and refusal (Lewis, 2001). Hence, approaches to implement lean concepts are already doomed to failure in case of employees do not actively cooperate. Last but not least, employees are the main drivers for changes with the power to enhance or avoid these very ones.

In addition, companies loose money if employees do not perform at their best. For lean managers this means motivating employees to perform at 100% - every percentage below is waste and inefficiency and ought to be improved (Lewis, 2001). But unlike expected, many hospitals still lack executive potential and strategic management of human resources. Oftentimes, the HR department solely consists of a wage and salary administration although innovative employment planning and development is needed and would help to reactivate idle human capital (Braun von Reinersdorff, 2007).

4.1.2 Requirements for Managers

Hospitals with the aim to implement lean concepts are definitely in need of a proper management who knows best about the previously described situation. Besides being well grounded in the management concept, managers shall possess certain qualifications, so-called soft skills. Soft skills are key competencies that depend on personal characteristics and individual behaviour. According to Lüthy and Schmiemann (2004), successful leaders must fall back on the ability to assert, decide, cooperate, work in team, accept criticism, communicate, resolve conflicts and organise. These soft skills enable managers to create and maintain a positive working climate with satisfied and motivated manpower that happily accepts and supports suggestions. By nature, hospitals are enormously complex organisations with hierarchic structures. On the one hand, this hierarchy is important for clear and unambiguous allocation of duties and fields of responsibility. On the other hand, the hierarchic hospital structure is exactly the reason why managers face biases within the hierarchy and among highly specialised and well-trained staff (especially at higher levels and in particular with senior physicians)[3] when making the attempt of introducing new concepts and ideas. For a continuous improvement process it is essential to overcome these biases and to achieve common acceptance among staff.

4.1.3 Motivation Methods

The creation of a solid employee base already starts with hiring new staff members. In chapter 3.3 Hospital Marketing, it has been examined how public relations can be used to create a positive image with the aim to attract patients. As a positive side effect, hospitals can benefit from such a positive image when hiring employees – á la *best attracts best*. During job interviews, where only most qualified and best suitable candidates are invited to, potential staff members shall receive the company as the ideal work place they feel even more attracted to work for (Lewis, 2001).

---

[3] To underline this statement, interviews with leading physicians, healthcare consultants and hospital quality managers were held by the author in December 2008.

After the hiring process, managers must ensure that employees receive a structured and comprehensive orientation and briefing into their job duties. The period of professional adjustment is very cost and time intensive whereas the latter is a real challenge for managers. Particularly the information flow is one of the determining factors that can strongly influence the motivational level of employees. To overcome the time problem managers shall partially delegate and empower one colleague of the same department to support the new staff member during the training period.

But how can managers increase motivation among existing staff to create modern loyalty and to avoid job burnout? Above all, managers must create a work environment that is based on trust and respect.

Managing without trust and respect is almost impossible and has a considerable impact on the economic activities and success of a company (Sprenger, 2005). Trust and respect evolve from appreciation managers are able to show employees and from their admission to let employees state their views and opinions as well as to communicate positive and negative feelings. In this context, the handling of fears gains importance. Lean managers accept that mistakes belong to human behaviour and can also present a chance for improvement and further optimisation of performances. Only with a solid basis of trust and respect managers can successfully motivate employees to increase their work performance. In general, there are two ways how employees can be motivated: by extrinsic and intrinsic motivation. External incentives such as basic salary, pay rise, cash incentives, bonuses and commissions, but also promotion and compliments belong to extrinsic motivation. Extrinsic motivation is not limited to financial aids because performance-related salary also enables people to reach and maintain a certain social status and to boost self-respect among colleagues and in privacy. In contrast, intrinsic motivation strongly refers to the affectivity of a person. It is rather a reward from inside and is characterised by satisfaction. Therefore, intrinsic motivation is bound to individual ideals and expectations, which enable a person to identify him or her with the work. Ideally, these expectations and personal traits are concordant with the activities of the person's professional life. Leaders shall create an incentive system that covers both aspects of motivation.

To further improve the morale and motivation level of staff managers should consider the following aspects (Lewis, 2001: 14-15):

- creation of a common vision and mission,
- encouragement of an open communication,
- enhancement of creativity and productivity,
- development of a suggestion system,
- design of a proper balance between empowerment and support,
- creation of an interesting incentive system,
- organisation of an appropriate recognition and reward system, and
- training and further training.

First, the creation of a common vision and mission immensely strengthens the corporate feeling of a company. Managers should succeed in aligning single interests and different energies of employees with the aim to reach a common objective. This objective can be perfectly modifiable or reachable by sub-ordinate targets. Suitable motivation measures are coaching, mentoring or auditing. Since auditing is especially interesting for lean hospitals it will be elaborated explicitly in chapter 4.3. Second, companies must comprise a sound information and communication system that enables employees to participate. In this context, the already described telemedicine concept shall be considered.

Leaders should encourage an open communication throughout the whole organisation including cross-functional areas, departments and staff levels (Lewis, 2001). Open communication ensures knowledge flow and subsequent synergy effects can be used. Third, managers should emphasise creativity among employees because creativity enhances productivity and eventually the profitability of an organisation. Therefore, unnecessary restraints and limits ought to be eliminated and employees shall be motivated to play a role in the creative process. Daily team meetings, brainstorming or the development of a suggestion system are just a few examples how creativity can be supported. In this context, it is very important that managers find a proper balance between authority and empowerment. It goes without saying, that empowerment in a hospital surely does not refer to methods of treatment or medication. Instead, empowerment in hospitals means self-sustaining management of daily routines or trial and error activities during process optimisation.

In any case, managers must actively listen to employees and, if necessary, support them. To motivate employees to participate in an improvement process leadership should ideally install an appropriate incentive or reward system. However, "incentives should be carefully chosen to encourage behaviour that is consistent with the needs of the organisation and of the employee and other team members" (Lewis, 2001: 16). Hence, possible rewards do not only include cash incentives such as bonuses, but also intangible goods such extra leave days or internal promotion.

Last, training and further training (either as reward or generally offered) will increase the motivational level of staff as well. Positively promoted trainings have two advantages: first of all, employees receive approval for their work and get the feeling of being respected. Furthermore, hospitals will benefit from employees specialisation in the long run. Thus, trainings provide a win-win-situation for both the employees and the hospital.

4.1.4 Conflict Resolution

Apart from a positive working climate, conflicts are likely to appear in hospitals due to the already mentioned structural complexity and personnel intensity. This is especially true for the introduction of suggestion systems because different people have different expectations, ideas, opinions, proposals and demands they wish to turn into reality. In general, unsolved problems and conflicts negatively influence and hinder daily work routines. In particular, conflicts can endanger the entire improvement process because they lead to frustration and discouragement among staff. Therefore, managers must always have the aim to resolve conflicts and to avoid escalation (Lüthy & Schmiemann, 2004). The most suitable way to resolve conflicts is the open communication in a blame-free environment whereas the manager assumes the part of a mediator. But conflicts are not always carried out in public. Managers must have a keen sense of the general working atmosphere. One indicator for hidden conflicts might be for instance negative staff morale. Employee attitude surveys are a helpful tool to gain information about possible conflicts and hidden problems, and provide information about the satisfaction and motivation level of staff, which is indispensable for the implementation of Lean.

4.2 Employee Attitude Surveys

Satisfaction surveys among hospital staff can help enhancing the continuous improvement process that is necessary to streamline processes and to create operative excellence. In lean hospitals those surveys are especially suitable to identify critical areas (e. g. high death rates, bottle-neck capacities) and to show need for action (e. g. auditing, coaching). Carefully planned and effectively implemented surveys do not only deliver insights to employees needs and their satisfaction level but can also become a strategic tool in reaching long-term company goals. So, employee surveys have different functions, such as diagnosis, evaluation, control or intervention (2ask, 2008). They allow managers to gain an insight into the hospital's strengths and weaknesses, and deliver information for a comparison of the current and the target situation, for frequent checking of already implemented improvement tools and for undertaking corrective measures in running processes. No matter which function the survey has to fulfil, it is of prior importance that the top management of the hospital stands behind the project from the very beginning (Lüthy & Schmiemann, 2004). In the course of the last health care reforms in Germany, hospitals have been forced to publish quality reports in a 2-year cycle (Busse & Riesberg, 2005). In this context, it is very important that employee surveys do not degenerate into simple accessory instruments. In particular, negative results or weak points that are not followed up by improvement measures will have a negative boomerang effect raising employee discouragement and frustration. In contrast, positively adapted surveys can create an open-minded working environment, lead to quality improvement and increase the satisfaction level.

4.2.1 Setting the Right Target

Above all, the key for a successful survey is setting the right target. The target defines the comprehensiveness, time frame, target group, number of participants and the methodology of the overall survey (2ask, 2008).

In lean hospitals, possible targets top managers have to decide on may be the following:

- information about employee satisfaction and loyalty level (e. g. work climate),
- transparency of weak points employees are confronted with in their daily routines,

- improved communication among one hierarchy level as well as between management and subordinate personnel,
- increased identification of employees with the corporate philosophy and acceptance of the mission statement,
- higher acceptance of introduced processes or medical technology,
- enhanced innovation management and suggestion system, and
- deeper analysis of problems that have not been examined in detail.

Surveys can be carried out in different ways. Hospital leaders must decide about different modes at the survey initiation and define the project scale. Especially in large hospitals it is advisable to proceed department by department instead of initiating a comprehensive survey that covers the whole organisation but is difficult to control. Furthermore, it has to be decided on the execution. If the hospital displays for example a rather negative work climate it would be advisable to call in external experts. In any case, surveys must be carried out voluntarily and anonymously ensuring that no one will be able to determine the person's identity based on the answers provided (Lüthy & Schmiemann, 2004). Besides cost and time advantages, digital surveys are preferable to traditional questionnaires because people cannot be identified due to their handwriting.

4.2.2 Designing the Questionnaire

Most importantly, the target delivers the basis for the content of the questionnaire. Accordingly, questions shall be realigned to actual needs of employees at their working field (Lüthy & Schmiemann, 2004). If questions are formulated in a simple and unequivocal style the chance for answers that reflect reality increases automatically. It is important that participants can identify themselves with the questions and are not overstrained because employees will then refuse participation. Furthermore, it is advisable to have a mixture of standard and specific questions that give information about general conditions (e. g. the working climate) and very specific situations (e. g. a complex ICU situation). Professional questionnaires shall cover questions of various subject areas. Leaders or an extra called-up project team must ensure that the questions in every subject area have been formulated bearing in mind the pre-decided objective. Let's assume a hospital with a high fluctuation rate of staff. The hospital management initiates a survey with the main target to identify reasons for the high turnover rate. The idea is to concentrate on the current satisfaction and loyalty level of the employees since these two factors are the main drivers for deciding whether to stay with or to leave a company. In general, the survey can include closed and open questions.

The following 4-Cs-Method delivers an example of how closed questions covering relevant subject areas can be designed:

Table 2 – 4-Cs-Method

Commitment	Culture
1. Labour Organisation	5. Working Atmosphere
2. Satisfaction Level	6. Innovation & Creativity
3. Job Conditions	7. Reputation & Image
4. Career & Training	8. Ethical Principles
Communication	**Compensation**
9. Colleagues & Executives	12. Remuneration
10. Cross-Department	13. Social Benefits
11. Patients	14. Incentives

Source: own, following Lüthy & Schmiemann, 2004

The first subject area *Commitment* includes topics that shall give information about the general engagement of employees. Possible statements about the satisfaction level are:

1. Duties are arranged equally: stressful situations or unnecessary off-time are avoided.

2. I have enough time to do my job properly.

3. I can make good use of my skills and abilities.

4. My job leaves room to become acquainted with news and to study further.

The second C – *Culture* – covers aspects that deliver insights about how employees identify themselves with the company and how they estimate the image and reputation of the hospital. Possible statements that give an overview about the loyalty level are:

5. Employees at my department trust and respect each other.

6. I am encouraged to learn from my mistakes rather than being reprimanded for them.

7. The hospital has a good standing in public.

8. There is a good sense of moral among the people I work with.

Deliberately chosen questions in the *Communication* section can give answers about the information flow in the hospital and the attitude of employees towards supervisors and patients; and vice-versa. Possible statements are:

9.   The department manager has always an open ear to my concerns.
10. Problems and conflicts are discussed in an open-minded and blame-free environment.
11. Information necessary for my working area is always given in time.

Lately, managers shall not be afraid of asking questions about the *Compensation* satisfaction. Possible statements are:

12. I am fairly paid according to my performance.
13. Vacation days are sufficient.
14. The suggestion system offers adequate incentives.

Likewise the already presented patient survey, the creation of an importance-satisfaction-matrix is advisable for employee surveys as well. Thus, interviewees should not only evaluate their satisfaction level but also estimate the individual importance of each statement.

In addition, open questions that refer to specific situations both positive and negative in nature would be advisable. Examples are:

15. If you think of your current job situation, what annoys you most?
16. What do you like best about your working field?

Answers which are out of the ordinary give managers reason to ask further questions and to get to the bottom of possible conflicts or problems. The above-mentioned closed and open questions are only an extract of how managers can formulate their target-based ideas and to get an overview about the current satisfaction and loyalty level among staff.

4.2.3 Communicating Objectives

Creating a professional and comprehensive questionnaire is surely the basis to obtain answers that are value adding for the improvement process afterwards. But employees will not participate automatically and need to be motivated by hospital managers or project leaders. The communication of a previously determined common goal is an effective tool to increase the motivation level and consequently the return rate. This goal can be communicated via different information channels, such as team meetings, posters and black boards, announcements in the house organ, circular mails, and websites or even in individual interviews between managers and employees (Lüthy & Schmiemann, 2004). Employees shall be informed about the target, benefits, methods, course and timeframe of the survey so they can identify themselves with the campaign. The covering letter which accompanies the questionnaire is another motivating factor that should not be underestimated.

Herein, the following information shall be included to enhance employees' motivation to participate and to dispel remaining uncertainties (2ask, 2008: 31):

- individual greeting,
- target and benefits of the survey,
- contact persons in case of possible questions,
- instructional and general advise how to fill in the questionnaire,
- reference to anonymity and voluntary decision of participation,
- dead line, and
- gratitude and information about future procedure.

Employee attitude surveys arouse certain expectations that ought to be fulfilled. Managers must be aware that employees expect and need a feedback because surveys without any feedback will automatically lead to frustration and disappointment. Since survey analyses generally take a certain time the first feedback might be a letter of thanks or the release of first figures about participation. After careful analysis of all collected data the findings can be published. Besides presenting only pure results employees shall be informed about how these results are interpreted and possibly used for further measures (2ask, 2008). In case of subsequent improvement procedures, employees already know about the urgency and necessity of corrective measurements which influences positively their willingness to participate. Revealing results from successfully carried out surveys provide an excellent basis for future improvement activities and necessary corrective measures. Auditing is one approach how survey findings can be used in a continuous improvement process by successively going into detail, further involvement of staff and prudential course of action.

4.3 Auditing

As already examined, motivated and satisfied staff is the basis for successful imple-mentation of Lean. Hence, the development of an extended supply chain towards a learning system provides an excellent model how employees can be motivated to participate in the improvement process. Besides, or because of, high personnel intensity the healthcare sector is furthermore one of the most skill-intensive industries. International exhibitions and special conferences, such as the world's largest health-care trade show, the Arab Health in Dubai, or frequent expert meetings and discus-sion forums with specific topics, show the need for action to keep up with latest trends, state-of-the-art technology and improved operating and curing methods. Therefore, the central challenge for hospitals in the 21st century is the design of a learning system, which is actually the creation of a common knowledge pool within one supply chain to ensure work-flow-management and to enhance knowledge transfer (Braun von Reinersdorff, 2007). Managers in such a learning hospital have two main tasks: to intelligibly determine the knowledge modules and processes within the chain and to motivate people to participate in this learning system.

4.3.1 Hospital Environment

Unfortunately, hospitals display a very complex structure that aggravates improve-ment measurements. Different departments work independently and working condi-tions, satisfaction levels and process flows at each department can differ a lot. Hospital managers or external consultants face biases among hospital staff, espe-cially among chief physicians and experienced decision makers. Thus, there is a need for an intelligent approach towards the introduction of a daily lean management system in hospitals. One suitable tool to overcome the described problematic situa-tion is the design and introduction of process audits. Implemented in a correct way, they offer excellent opportunities for improvement. Furthermore, hospital leadership can create almost automatically a proper balance between control and empowerment of staff. In chapter 2, it has already been examined how processes can be optimised in a lean environment. This chapter deals with process optimisation from the human perspective because the key to successful process auditing is both the application of an elaborated model and the involvement of employees at all times and at any level.

4.3.2 The 6-Level-Model

One core element in auditing is the use of the 6-level-model. This model delivers an excellent guideline for hospitals to reach efficient management by systematic elimination of waste and losses at every below-mentioned level of the model (Leikep & Bieber, 2006: 21):

Table 3 6-Level-Model

Level	Quintessence	Target
1	Creation of a Proper Basis	Self-Organisation
2	Improvement	Cooperation
3	Economisation	Process Improvement
4	Maintenance of the Reached Level	Optimisation within the Team
5	Full Responsibility	Flexible Teamwork
6	Process Control	"Best in Class"

Source: own, following Leikep & Bieber, 2006

The creation of a proper basis is indispensable for the success of the whole process auditing. Above all, it is of prior importance that the top management stands behind the idea from the very beginning and demonstrates mutual agreement with the middle management and executing personnel. Moreover, top managers must decide on the extensiveness of the project. For beginners or in large hospitals, it is advisable to start department by department not to loose control. The core activity of this stage is to retrieve waste and inefficiency. Thus, supervisors have the critical role to motivate and encourage staff to participate and to learn how to recognise waste (Dickmann, 2006). Above all, staff can be motivated and encouraged to participate by communicating a common goal that is clear and reasonable for all participating members. A simple but effective tool is letting employees agree on a name or headline for the process auditing, so they can identify themselves with the action. From the very beginning, it must be clear that the search for waste and inefficiency does not aim at blaming people for existing grievances. Instead, it is the search for processes and conditions that need to be improved. In this context, employees must be trained to distinguish between value-adding and non-value adding activities (Leikep & Bieber, 2006). In hospitals, value adding activities are suggestions and ideas that contribute to improvement of safety, quality, time and costs. Here, managers shall explain the goal, set objectives and limits, and support staff to achieve the goals. It is

very important that employees do not associate redundancies or momentous consequences for the advance in their position. Audits can be carried out by standardised
questionnaires that contain certain score levels to be reached for further work flow.
Only if a certain score level is reached, the next level can be initiated.

Level 2 has the target to improve cooperation. This goal can be reached by clear
communication and the introduction of standards (Leikep & Bieber, 2006). Managers
must ensure at any time and under any circumstances that the information flow works
among the hospital staff. One option to ensure information flow is the introduction of
checklists (Dickmann, 2006). Checklists can include standard questions and particular questions that are valid for the respective department and can therefore be
regarded standards within the particular department or activity area. By setting
standards, waste of time for searching items is abolished and transparency increases
whereas employees are enabled to concentrate on their core work. With regard to
sterile goods or drugs the existence of a *shine* workplace becomes even more
important. But managers might be confronted with the fact that people are afraid to
write down problems. Therefore, it is very important that employees are encouraged
intensively to state their honest opinion about processes and conditions that ought to
be improved. By letting the team establish and decide about standards and rules,
people are involved and therefore motivated to participate at this level. Especially
front-line employees can deliver real treasures managers would not have been able
to consider from their perspective. Again, this level is concluded with an auditing to
ensure that the set standards and rules have been established and implemented
successfully.

In level 3, work processes are examined more intensively because the improvement
of processes bears excellent economisation opportunities (Leikep & Bieber, 2006). In
hospitals, this is especially true with regard to patient-flow optimisation. Managers
must get an accurate picture about daily workflow and processes which enables
them to further encourage employees to continue with standardised procedures or, if
necessary, to undertake corrective actions. For long-term success, managers must
measure all performances and shall have control at any time and under any circumstances. In a large hospital this might be a challenge and means that managers have
to rely on reporting supervisors or any other assigned personnel. Two methods to

gain more transparency among processes are process mapping and problem solution techniques (Leikep & Bieber, 2006). Process mapping is the continuous checking of existing standards and the further minimisation of waste by concentrating on the basics. It is very important that managers evaluate every single suggestion brought forward by employees in a positive way. Even if the suggestion is inappropriate managers must think about why this idea was brought forward (Graban, 2008). In many cases, the source problem is the real cost driver and only an alternative solution must be found. Or if the solution suggestion does not fulfil expectations, managers know at least that no further efforts shall be undertaken. Regarding problem solution techniques, the method of asking 5-whys is a suitable tool to come to the initial problem and, consequently, to find the appropriate solution.

During level 4, the maintenance of already reached results and the optimisation thereof is of main interest. With visual management and the set of goals employees will be motivated to keep on searching for improvement (Leikep & Bieber, 2006). It is a misbelieve that auditing is already finished with level 3 – instead, further efforts must be undertaken to ensure that the optimisation process is continued so the whole auditing process does not end in a blind alley. A supporting tool for motivation is the design of metrics. Metrics should be visible, visual and statistically meaningful. It is very important that the metric board is placed in the department where every employee has easy access to it and can see the board without any problem during daily routines. By having daily stand-up team meetings employees can be engaged to identify themselves with the optimisation process and to continue participating in the project. For leaders it is very important to use metrics and to identify failures and negative trends in a blame-free environment (Graban, 2008). Thus, findings of metrics must never be personalised but rather present trends of how processes are performing. Considering the described impersonal course of action, meetings in front of the metric board are advantageous to anonymous problem suggestion boxes because they deliver immediate suggestions. However, team meetings in front of metrics should not take longer than 10 minutes because the main intention is quick communication around immediate needs and not detailed discussion or even problem solving (Dickmann, 2006).

Quick metrics communication leads directly to the next level where employees take full responsibility for their suggestions put into action. New concepts are tested, adopted, modified or abandoned. Thus, leaders must distinguish simple fluctuations from trends to be followed and considered for further improvement. Employees are empowered to find their best suitable ways for work process optimisation. Again, it is very important that all actions are carried out in a positively experimental and blame-free environment. The role of the leader is setting a framework, supervising all actions carried out by employees within the set framework, enhancing employees to participate, lending a helping hand to everyone who is in need of and, if necessary, undertaking corrective actions. One motivator is the formulation of objectives. These objectives might be common goals, intermediate goals, team goals or even a business strategy (Leikep & Bieber, 2006). In hospitals, all goals should be backed up with the intention to improve safety, quality, delivery, costs and morale (Graban, 2008). Possibly, not all goals are applicable in every department or activity field due to structural or work flow conditions. Thus, leaders must identify the best applicable measures for the corresponding department and activity field. This level is completed with an auditing from which one priority emerges: the achievement of operative excellence of the department or hospital.

With the achievement of level 5 the hospital has gained the status of a first-quality lean healthcare provider. In level 6 – Process Control – the focus lies on external conditions. Whilst internal processes are further controlled benchmarking gains more and more importance. Especially in our globalised world, it is important to be one step ahead to ones competitors. There are many benchmarking opportunities for hospitals. By way of example, they can learn from other healthcare providers in an international context. In Germany, needed transparency for comparison is given due to the last healthcare reforms (Busse & Riesberg, 2005). Furthermore, the internet provides easy access to information that promotes benchmarking. Expert congresses and meetings, continuing educational opportunities at universities or institutions enable managers to meet the demands by specialising and further training and to frequently challenge the status quo of the rapidly changing healthcare sector conditions.

5. Conclusion

Lean is an improvement strategy that concentrates on waste-free production and process optimisation. For lean leaders, it is indispensable to identify, analyse and categorise existing types of waste to successfully elaborate a strategy for breaking the cycle of waste. Hospitals are complex business environments with a multitude of wasteful situations that require distinctive solution approaches. Kanban, Kaizen, 5S-principle and Value Stream Mapping are adequate tools that help to identify and eliminate waste and non-value adding activities. However, certain problems may remain unresolved or difficult systems and structures are too complex to be stream-lined with lean principles only. This is the moment, when Lean Sigma comes into play because with Six Sigma the lean methodology is supported by error proofing and future avoidance thereof. Since the healthcare environment is a fast driving business field, state-of-the art technology such as telemedicine and e-health become more and more important. Besides the main goal of cost reduction, telemedicine further enables hospitals to cope with international competition and to fulfil current demands of EU standards and regulations within the European Single Market.

Furthermore, patient-oriented management is another priority of lean management in hospitals. It helps hospitals to concentrate on their core competencies and to avoid ineffective and inefficient activities. Above all, patient satisfaction and loyalty are important for the continuity and profitability of a hospital. To increase this satisfaction and loyalty level, hospitals must stand out from its competitors by differentiation. This calls for a comprehensive analysis of the company's resources and capabilities as well as for the understanding of patient demands. As a result, strategic alliances gain interest because it turned out that strategic alliances are one possibility for hospitals to cope with harsh market conditions. Thus, hospitals can expand their service portfolio without additional financial costs; they can concentrate simultaneously on their core competencies and follow trends by streamlining their activities according to patient demands; they can increase their profitability and efficiency without personnel cutbacks. Moreover, any business cooperation should also be supported by profes-sional marketing. In times of increasing competition and changing patient self-conception, hospitals cannot afford to neglect marketing activities that help to stick into customers' minds.

Last but not least, employees play a key role for successful implementation of lean concepts in hospitals since satisfied and motivated staff is more likely to participate in improvement processes. Accordingly, leaders must spare no efforts to elaborate suitable tools for the creation and maintenance of a positive working climate. Employee attitude surveys are one suitable tool to gain information about the general working atmosphere. Most importantly, surveys can reveal problematic situations and conflicts that ought to be eliminated. Furthermore, surveys give managers the opportunity to increase and retain a certain satisfaction and motivation level that provides a solid basis for further improvement measures, such as auditing. Although auditing is a complex and time-intensive management tool, it can be regarded an excellent way to implement lean concepts in hospitals because it enables managers to guide employees in a constructive manner whereas the hospital will benefit in the long-run.

Summing up, it can be stated that key factors for successful implementation of lean management in hospitals are concentration on process optimisation, knowledge about main lean principles and intelligent application of its general tools. For Lean to tap its full potential, the human aspect must be considered likewise. Thus, a patient-oriented management as well as engaging and leading employees will lead to success of lean management in the healthcare environment.

Taking all aspects of into consideration lean management will considerably contribute to fulfil the Hippocratic Oath whereas physicians and other hospital staff are enabled and positively enhanced to

"...follow that system of regimen which, according to their ability and judgement, they consider for the benefit of their patients, and abstain from whatever is deleterious and mischievous..."

6. Appendices

Appendix 1

Value Stream Mapping of Typical Patient Flow in a Haematology Department

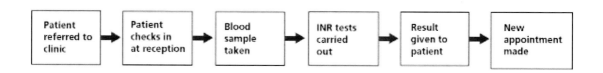

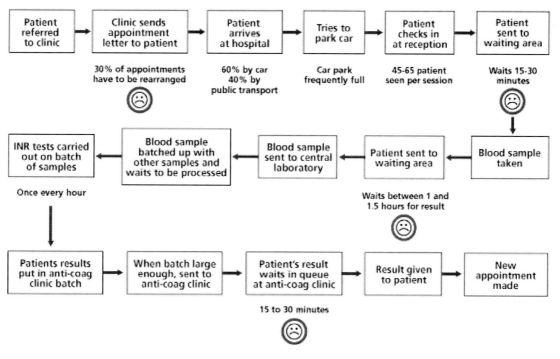

THE ANTICOAGULANT BLOOD TESTING PROCESS

 Effect on the patient

Source: NHS UK, 2008

Appendix 2

EURO HEALTH CONSUMER INDEX 2007

Legend:
- ● = Good
- ◑ = Intermediary
- ○ = Poor
- n.a. = Data not available

SUBDISCIPLINE	INDICATOR
Patient rights and information	Healthcare law based on Patient Rights
	Patient org. involved in decision making
	No-fault malpractice insurance
	Right to second opinion
	Access to own medical record
	Register of legit doctors
	Electronic Patient Record (% of GPs using)
	Provider catalogue with quality ranking
	Web or 24/7 telephone healthcare info
	Subdiscipline score
Waiting times	Family doctor same day
	Direct access to specialist
	Major non-acute operations <90 days
	Cancer therapy < 21 days
	MR exam < 7 days
	Subdiscipline score
Outcomes	Heart infarct mortality
	Infant deaths / 1000 live births
	Cancer 5-year survival
	Avoidable deaths – Potential years of Life Lost PYLL/100 000
	MRSA infections
	Subdiscipline score
"Generosity" of public healthcare systems	Cataract operations per 100 000
	Infant 4-disease vaccination
	Kidney transplants p.m.p.
	Dental care in public health care system
	Subdiscipline score
Pharmaceuticals	Rx subsidy %
	Layman-adapted pharmacopoeia?
	New cancer drugs deployment speed
	Access to new drugs (time to subsidy)
	Subdiscipline score
	TOTAL SCORE
	RANK

Health Consumer Powerhouse
www.healthpowerhouse.com

7. Bibliography

Albaum, G., Strandskov, J., & Duerr, E. (2001). *Internationales Marketing und Exportmanagement* (3rd ed.). Munich, Germany: Pearson Education Deutschland GmbH.

Becker, H.-D. (2008, October 29). *Session 10 – Qualification Stays for Physicians, Nurses and Paramedics.* 3rd German-Arab Health Forum. Chamber of Commerce Hamburg. Hamburg, Germany.

Braun von Reinersdorff, A. (2007). *Strategische Krankenhausführung. Vom Lean Managment zum Balanced Hospital Management* (2nd ed.). Bern, Switzerland: Verlag Hans Huber, Hogrefe AG.

Buckley, P. T. (2007). *Complete Guide to Hospital Marketing.* Marblehead, USA: Opus Communication. Retrieved October 10, 2008 from http://www.hcmarketplace.com /supplemental/5352_browse.pdf.

Bundesärztekammer (2006). Retrieved October 12, 2008, from http://www.bundesaerztekammer.de/ page.asp?his=1.100.1143#B42.

Busse, R., Riesberg, A. (2005). *Gesundheitssysteme im Wandel.* Berlin, Germany: Mwv Medizinisch Wissenschaftliche Verlagsgesellschaft OHG.

Dickmann, P. (2006). *Schlanker Materialfluss mit Lean Production, Kanban und Innovationen.* Berlin, Germany: Springer-Verlag.

Edelstein, L. (1943). *From The Hippocratic Oath: Text, Translation, and Interpretation.* Baltimore, USA: Johns Hopkins Press.

Euractiv (2008). E-Health – Elektronische Gesundheitsdienste. Retrieved December 18, 2008, from http://www.euractiv.com/de/gesundheit/e-health-elektronische-gesundheitdienste/ article-103635.

Geiger, D. (2008). *Jahrbuch Healthcare Marketing 2008*. Hamburg, Germany: New Business Verlag GmbH & Co. KG.

Graban, M. (2008). *Lean Hospitals. Improving Quality, Patient Safety, and Employee Satisfaction*. New York, USA: Taylor & Francis Group, LLC.

Health Powerhouse Web site. (2007). Retrieved April 26, 2008, from http://www.healthpowerhouse.com /media/Rapport_EHCI_2007.pdf.

Heskett, J. (2003). *Shouldice Hospital Limited*. Boston, USA: Harvard Business School Publishing.

Heskett, J. L., Sasser, W. Earl Jr., Schlesinger, L. A. (1997). *The Service Profit Chain*. New York, USA: The Free Press.

isixsigma (2008). Retrieved on December 1, 2008 from http://www.isixsigma.com/ library/content/sigma_table.asp.

isixsigma (2008). Retrieved on December 1, 2008 from http://healthcare.isixsigma.com/ library/content/c040526a.asp

Jahrbuch Healthcare Marketing 2008. Hamburg, Germany: New Business Verlag GmbH & Co. KG.

Jones, D. & Mitchell, A. (2006). *Lean Thinking for the NHS*. London, UK: NHS Confederation.

Kusitzky, A., Schuster, J. (2008). Patient 1. Klasse. 20 unverzichtbare Antworten. (2008, September 15). *Focus*, 38, p. 74.

Leikep, S., Bieber, K. (2006). *Der Weg. Effizienz im Büro mit KAIZEN-Methoden* (2nd ed.). Norderstedt, Germany: Books on Demand GmbH.

Lewis A. G. (2001). *Streamlining health care operations: how lean logistics can transform health care organizations*. San Francisco, USA: The Jossey-Bass / AHA Press).

Liker, J. K. (2003). *The Toyota Way*. New York, USA: Mc Graw-Hill Companies.

Lüthy A., Schmiemann J. (2004). *Mitarbeiterorientierung im Krankenhaus. Soft Skills erfolgreich umsetzen*. Stuttgart, Germany: W. Kohlhammer Druckerei GmbH+ Co Stuttgart.

Mayer, A. G. (2005). *Marktorientierung im Krankenhaus der Zukunft*. Kulmbach, Germany: Baumann Fachverlage GmbH & Co. KG.

Müller, N., Kossack, K., Gröfke, G. (2008). *Jahrbuch Healthcare Marketing 2008*. Hamburg, Germany: New Business Verlag GmbH & Co. KG.

NHS Web site (2008). Retrieved November 20, 2008 from http://www.nodelaysachiever. nhs.uk/NR/rdonlyres/F87F3BCF-AB3B-4D06-B791-1A8567B41D6E/0/231b.gif.

Norris, A. C. (2002). *Essentials of Telemedicine and Telecare*. West Sussex, UK: John Wiley & Son, Ltd.

Orlowski, U., Wasem, J. (2007). *Gesundheitsreform 2007 (GKV-WSG): Änderungen und Auswirkungen auf einen Blick*. Heidelberg, Germany: Müller (C.F.Jur.).

Patienten fassen Vertrauen in Roboter-Operationen: Gute Erfahrung bei Prostata-Eingriffen in Hamburg. (2008, October 8). Ärzte Zeitung [online].

Reimann, A. (2007, 18 April). *Prozess in Berlin. Der Todesengel im Glaskasten*. Retrieved January 3, 2009 from http://www.spiegel.de/panorama/justiz/0,1518,477959,00.html.

Schönermark, M. P. (2007, November 12). *Lean Health Care – Principles and Practice.* 2nd German-Arab Health Forum. Chamber of Commerce Berlin. Berlin, Germany.

Sprenger, R. K, (2005). *Die besten Management-Tools 2: Personal und Führung.* Frankfurt/Main, Germany: Campus Verlag GmbH.

Stanslowski, J. (2008). *Überleben durch Strategische Allianzen.* Munich. Germany. Official Report of Sana Hospital AG retrieved November 20, 2008 from http://www.trillco.de/veranstaltung28022008/Vortrag8_Hr_Stanslowski.pdf.

Thompson, D. (1995). *The Concise Oxford Dictionary of Current English* (9th ed.).New York, USA: Oxford University Press.

Trusko, B. E., Pexton, C., Harrington, H. J. & Gupta, P. (2007). *Improving Healthcare Quality and Cost with Six Sigma.* New Jersey, USA: Pearson Education Inc.

Wende, S. (2008). *Strategische Allianzen in Deutschen Krankenhäusern. Eine empirische Analyse.* Saarbrücken, Germany: VDM Verlag Dr. Müller AG & Co. KG.

Ziesche, A. (2008). *Patientenzufriedenheit im Krankenhaus. Maßnahmen zur Verbesserung.* Bremen, Germany: CT Salzwasser-Verlag GmbH & Co. KG.

2ask (2008). Retrieved November 18, 2008, from http://www.2ask.de/media/1/10/2/3/5/ 049809ac62c5a529/Leitfaden_Mitarbeiterbefragung.pdf.

Danksagung

An dieser Stelle möchte ich mich bei Prof. Dr. Rüdiger Heinemann, Dekan der European Management School in Leipzig, bedanken, der mit seiner anspruchsvollen und menschlichen Motivation wesentlich zum Gelingen der Arbeit beigetragen und der Betreuung eine besondere moralische Dimension verliehen hat.

Von Herzen danke ich meinem Mann Stephan Lindenau für seine unermüdliche Geduld und Liebe in den schwierigen Zeiten des „Nachtstudiums".

Author

Verena Lindenau-Stockfisch was born on February 6, 1976 in Meißen (Saxony) and grew up in the today's known New Laender in Germany. After her graduation as an International Management Assistant in 2003, she was working in an export company, specialised on turn-key hospital projects mainly in the Middle East. In 2009, she graduated from her extra-occupational but full-time BA studies that were important to improve her professional skills in the fields of Business Administration. Various stays abroad, among others in Great Britain and South Africa, as well as the BA studies mainly held in English, contributed to her language skills and enabled her to work on an academic level.

Already during her work as a Project Manager, she gained comprehensive experience with regard to structuring, elaboration and budgeting of international hospital projects. Above all, her position demanded the ability of leading a project team and cooperation with engineers, medical planners and architects and to ensure optimal process structuring in a hospital from the very beginning. At a German-Arabic Health & Economy Congress in 2006, she became first acquainted with the definition Lean Healthcare. Since that day, she has been fascinated and intensively studied the topic Lean Management in Hospitals. Since January 2011, Ms Lindenau-Stockfisch has been working for a hospital near Leipzig. In her position as a Manager for Strategic Planning she is accepting the challenge of introducing and implementing the Lean Methodology there.